Arms, Transparency and Security in South-East Asia

Stockholm International Peace Research Institute

SIPRI is an independent institute for research into problems of peace and conflict, especially those of arms control and disarmament. It was established in 1966 to commemorate Sweden's 150 years of unbroken peace.

The Institute is financed mainly by the Swedish Parliament. The staff and the Governing Board are international. The Institute also has an Advisory Committee as an international consultative body.

The Governing Board is not responsible for the views expressed in the publications of the Institute.

Governing Board

Professor Daniel Tarschys, Chairman (Sweden)
Dr Oscar Arias Sánchez (Costa Rica)
Dr Ryukichi Imai (Japan)
Professor Catherine Kelleher (United States)
Dr Marjatta Rautio (Finland)
Dr Lothar Rühl (Germany)
Dr Abdullah Toukan (Jordan)
The Director

Director

Dr Adam Daniel Rotfeld (Poland)

Stockholm International Peace Research Institute
Frösunda, S-171 53 Solna, Sweden
Telephone: 46 8/655 97 00
Telefax: 46 8/655 97 33
Email: sipri@sipri.se
Internet URL: http://www.sipri.se

Arms, Transparency and Security in South-East Asia

SIPRI Research Report No. 13

Edited by

Bates Gill and J. N. Mak

OXFORD UNIVERSITY PRESS
1997

Oxford University Press, Great Clarendon Street, Oxford OX2 6DP

Oxford New York Athens Auckland Bangkok Bogotá Bombay
Buenos Aires Calcutta Cape Town Dar es Salaam
Delhi Florence Hong Kong Istanbul Karachi
Kuala Lumpur Madras Madrid Melbourne
Mexico City Nairobi Paris Singapore
Taipei Tokyo Toronto
and associated companies in
Berlin Ibadan

Oxford is a trade mark of Oxford University Press

Published in the United States
by Oxford University Press Inc., New York

British Library Cataloguing in Publication Data
Data available
Library of Congress Cataloguing-in-Publication Data
Data available

ISBN 0–19–829285–6
ISBN 0–19–829286–4 (pbk)

Typeset and originated by Stockholm International Peace Research Institute
Printed in Great Britain on acid-free paper by Biddles Ltd,
Guildford and King's Lynn

Contents

Preface

Transparency and information sharing on defence-related matters are gaining ground throughout the international community as legitimate and useful means to enhance confidence and security among nations. Such efforts seem particularly prudent in South-East Asia where an arms build-up is in progress—the result of the uncertainty of the post-cold war regional security framework, increased economic resources and efforts to make up for long delays in military modernization.

The Stockholm International Peace Research Institute (SIPRI) is therefore pleased to offer this volume as a contribution to the nascent debate in South-East Asia on the development of region-based defence-related transparency and information-sharing mechanisms. This study offers conceptual and factual tools related to arms, transparency and security in South-East Asia which practitioners and specialists can use to shape their discussions and policies towards consensus and common goals. The authors tend to agree that it is too early to formalize transparency in the form of a regional arms register or other obligatory submissions at the official level. However, the time is ripe and South-East Asia is an appropriate place to make concrete progress at the official and the unofficial level by exploring the conceptual and practical possibilities for transparency and data sharing as a means to build confidence and security among regional neighbours.

The book emerges from a cooperative effort between SIPRI and the Maritime Institute of Malaysia (MIMA) dating from June 1995, which has included exchanges of persons and data between the two institutes, the publication of *ASEAN Arms Acquisitions: Developing Transparency* and *East Asian Maritime Arms Acquisitions: A Database of East Asian Naval Arms Imports and Production 1975–1996*, and the MIMA-supported workshop on arms trade transparency held in Kuala Lumpur in October 1995. The cooperative spirit which motivates this work draws on the respective strengths and shared goals the two institutes bring to the relationship.

Adam Daniel Rotfeld
Director of SIPRI
December 1996

Acknowledgements

This work results from the generous support of several individuals and research centres. First and foremost we are extremely grateful for the support of our two institutes, SIPRI and MIMA, and their directors, Dr Adam Daniel Rotfeld and Dr B. A. Hamzah, respectively. They have provided us with stimulating intellectual environments and logistical support, without which this volume could not have been completed.

We also wish to thank our fellow contributors, whose collegiality and insight over the years have broadened our horizons intellectually and made the burdens of editorship far less taxing than they could have been. Among these contributors, Siemon T. Wezeman and the SIPRI Arms Transfers Project have played a particularly critical role in supporting the SIPRI–MIMA cooperation. In addition, this work greatly benefited from the critical comments of several reviewers, including Ian Anthony, Malcolm Chalmers, Timothy Huxley, Ravinder Pal Singh and Matthew Stephenson. Dr Hamzah and MIMA deserve special thanks for hosting the October 1995 workshop in Kuala Lumpur, at which the chapters offered here were first presented. MIMA also supported the publication in August 1995 of the MIMA–SIPRI report *ASEAN Arms Acquisitions: Developing Transparency*.

The editors of this work at SIPRI, Eve Johansson and Connie Wall, and Rebecka Charan, editorial assistant, provided substantive improvements and polish to the manuscript. As research editors and co-authors of this volume, we thankfully acknowledge all these important contributions, but accept responsibility for any deficiencies which remain.

We hope that our cooperative efforts can serve to stimulate other joint programmes among leading research institutes aimed at sustaining stability and prosperity in South-East Asia and the Asia–Pacific region.

Bates Gill   J. N. Mak
SIPRI, Stockholm   MIMA, Kuala Lumpur

Acronyms

AAM	Air-to-air missile
APC	Armoured personnel carrier
ARF	ASEAN Regional Forum
ASEAN	Association of South-East Asian Nations
ASM	Air-to-surface missile
BTWC	Biological and Toxin Weapons Convention
CBM	Confidence-building measure
CFE	Conventional Armed Forces in Europe
COCOM	Coordinating Committee (on Multilateral Export Controls)
CSCAP	Council for Security Cooperation in the Asia Pacific
CSCE	Conference on Security and Co-operation in Europe
CSIS	Center for Strategic and International Studies
CWC	Chemical Weapons Convention
EEZ	Exclusive economic zone
MIMA	Maritime Institute of Malaysia
MTCR	Missile Technology Control Regime
NPT	Non-Proliferation Treaty
OSCE	Organization for Security and Co-operation in Europe
SAM	Surface-to-air missile
SLOC	Sea line of communication
SSM	Surface-to-surface missile
UNCDA	UN Centre for Disarmament Affairs
UNCLOS	UN Convention on the Law of the Sea
UNROCA	United Nations Register of Conventional Arms
ZOPFAN	Zone of Peace, Freedom and Neutrality

1. Introduction

Bates Gill and J. N. Mak

I. Setting the scene

The dynamism of South-East Asia in terms of multilateral diplomacy, economic growth, social change and military modernization both promises the possibilities of stable prosperity and threatens the outbreak of troubling tensions. The critical task for its leaderships and citizenry in the years ahead will be to put that dynamism to work in order to manage political, economic, social and military transformation in ways that are conducive to stability and prosperity.

The issues of arms, transparency and security in South-East Asia are intricately interwoven with the larger dynamics of change in the region.[1] In no small measure these issues will affect the outcomes, peaceful or otherwise, of the region's complex interactions. In recognition of this, in recent years a nascent effort has emerged among official and unofficial observers concerned with South-East Asian security to consider whether and how openness and transparency in arms and defence-related matters might serve as a confidence-building and security-enhancing measure in South-East Asia and in the Asia–Pacific region more broadly.[2]

A number of official statements, seminars and working papers have resulted from this effort, but these have most often been too dismissive, too ambitious or lacking in conceptual depth, practical recommendations and alternative approaches. Little in the way of concrete suggestions has emerged at either the official or the unofficial level in South-East Asia. There are, moreover, three arguments often heard in the region against the development of transparency.

First, some argue that transparency goes too far in revealing sensitive information and military secrets and as a result undermines, rather than enhances, stability and security. This view too easily ignores the

---

[1] Throughout this book, unless otherwise indicated, 'arms' refers to conventional weapons.

[2] Throughout this book, unless otherwise indicated, 'South-East Asia' is defined to include Brunei, Cambodia, Indonesia, Laos, Malaysia, Myanmar, the Philippines, Singapore, Thailand and Viet Nam. 'Asia–Pacific' refers to the countries of South-East Asia plus Australia, Canada, China, Japan, North Korea, South Korea, Mongolia, New Zealand, Russia, Papua New Guinea, Taiwan and the United States.

fact that a vast amount of information on arms and defence-related issues already exists in the open literature as well as among intelligence sources. Moreover, properly developed and implemented, transparency and information sharing are not so much about 'bean-counting' and quantitative assessments as about the mutually perceived need to build confidence and understanding among countries in an uncertain and often insecure world.

Second, the need for greater defence-related transparency is often dismissed as irrelevant in South-East Asia, a region which already enjoys considerable stability, prosperity and a growing sense of community. Yet it is precisely the unique methods of conducting diplomacy in South-East Asia which could leave the region ill-prepared to manage the new security challenges of the post-cold war era. Appropriate levels of openness and information sharing on arms and defence issues could strengthen the relatively stable security environment in the region and help regional states to develop a more effective security community for the future.

Third, transparency for transparency's sake or the wholesale and uncritical adoption of frameworks and policies developed outside the region seem ill-suited to addressing region-based problems and will be rejected as foreign and inapplicable to regional realities.

Into this breach must be introduced a greater understanding of basic concepts, conditions and possible pragmatic approaches regarding arms, transparency and security in South-East Asia. However, the available literature to date contains very few systematic and comprehensive efforts to explore the basic problems, policies and prospects for developing greater transparency in South-East Asia or to study how or whether such openness and information sharing might contribute to security in the region.[3]

In seeking to fill these gaps in the understanding of South-East Asian security, this book addresses three fundamental questions:

---

[3] One recent work which develops these themes in some depth is Chalmers, M., *Confidence-Building in South-East Asia*, Bradford Arms Register Studies no. 6 (Westview Press: Boulder, Colo., 1996), especially pp. 171–214, 221–27. See also Gill, B., Mak, J. N. and Wezeman, S. (eds), *ASEAN Arms Acquisitions: Developing Transparency* (MIMA: Kuala Lumpur, Aug. 1995); and Cossa, R. A. (ed.), *Toward a Regional Arms Register in the Asia Pacific*, Pacific Forum CSIS Occasional Papers Series (Pacific Forum CSIS [Center for Strategic and International Studies]: Honolulu, Aug. 1995).

1. What conceptual frameworks give shape to efforts to develop transparency measures on arms and defence-related matters in South-East Asia?

2. What current strategic and political conditions and policies in South-East Asia either support or undermine movement towards transparency in South-East Asia?

3. What initial pragmatic and security-enhancing steps might be taken towards developing greater transparency in South-East Asia?

Taken together, the contributions to this volume offer some initial responses to these queries and seek to advance the debate in South-East Asia on openness and information sharing related to arms and defence matters.

II. Basic principles and definitions

Linking transparency to security

Three core principles infuse the contributions to this volume. First and most important among these is the belief that properly developed transparency measures can make an effective and sustained contribution to improving security among neighbours in the international community and in South-East Asia in particular. This principle rests squarely on the understandings that such a process can in itself serve as a confidence-building measure (CBM) and that such openness will help to clarify intentions, dispel suspicions and open new avenues for cooperation, laying the groundwork for trust and improved relations.

Early on in the development of the United Nations Register of Conventional Arms (UNROCA), the world's foremost arms trade transparency mechanism, transparency was promoted 'so as to encourage prudent restraint by States in their arms exports and to reduce the risks of misunderstandings, suspicion or tension resulting from lack of information concerning arms transfers':[4]

Transparency could prevent exaggerated estimates by States that perceive a potential military threat from another country. By removing, or at least reducing, uncertainty about other States' arms transfers, arms races fuelled by misperceptions could be dampened and regional and international ten-

---

[4] United Nations, Study on ways and means of promoting transparency in international transfers of conventional arms (UN Office for Disarmament Affairs: New York, 1992), p. 3.

sions reduced . . . The defensive character of military structures and activities could also be emphasised. This could alleviate the security concerns of other States not directly related to arms transfers and could serve as a signal that there is a readiness for dialogue on security concerns.[5]

Considerably more theoretical and empirical work needs to be done to further delineate and explain the linkage between transparency and security, or between arms build-ups and the outbreak of instability. The work in this volume represents a step in this process, particularly as these efforts apply to South-East Asia.

The inclusive approach to transparency

A second important principle held by contributors to this volume is that transparency must be understood in an inclusive sense, to incorporate arms-related transparency mechanisms such as arms registers as well as consultative bodies to address arms build-ups, the sharing of defence-related information through such means as White Papers and other exchanges of militarily relevant information and data. This approach differs in many ways from others which place a too narrow emphasis on a United Nations-style arms trade register—an approach which is flawed in at least three important respects.

First, the UNROCA, in spite of its many successes, has a number of shortcomings as an arms-related transparency mechanism.[6] Perhaps most importantly, while it provides useful information, it does not provide for a consultative mechanism or forum in which the countries concerned can discuss and address the information available in the UNROCA. Second, the reporting categories of the UNROCA may not be well suited to the concerns of South-East Asia and it does not require reporting on current weapon holdings and domestic produc-

[5] United Nations (note 4), pp. 22–23.

[6] Comprehensive descriptions and evaluations of the UNROCA include Laurance, E. J. and Keith, T., 'The United Nations Register of Conventional Arms: on course in its third year of reporting', *Nonproliferation Review* (Mar. 1996); Laurance, E. J. and Wulf, H., 'The 1994 review of the UN Register of Conventional Arms', *SIPRI Yearbook 1995: Armaments, Disarmament and International Security* (Oxford University Press: Oxford, 1995), pp. 556–68; Chalmers, M. and Greene, O., *Taking Stock: The UN Register After Two Years* (Westview Press: Boulder, Colo., 1995); Chalmers, M. *et al.* (eds), *Developing the UN Register of Conventional Arms* (Department of Peace Studies, University of Bradford: Bradford, 1994); and Laurance, E. J., Wezeman, S. T. and Wulf, H., *Arms Watch: SIPRI Report on the First Year of the UN Register of Conventional Arms,* SIPRI Research Report no. 6 (Oxford University Press: Oxford, 1993).

tion.[7] Third, submissions are entirely voluntary and unenforceable, which means that states may freely choose not to participate.

Thus, wholesale adoption of the UNROCA or a similar arms trade register system would not meet region-specific arms trade concerns, nor would it adequately address concerns through the all-important vehicle of a consultative mechanism. The discussion in this volume recognizes these potential drawbacks and offers a more inclusive and flexible approach to what is meant by transparency in arms- and defence-related matters.

The significance of South-East Asia

The choice to focus this volume on South-East Asia illustrates a third principle shared by the contributors: that South-East Asia is particularly well suited as a region to achieve considerable progress in debates on openness and information sharing concerning arms and defence matters.

First, in December 1994, following the 1994 review of the UNROCA, the UN General Assembly voted to wait until 1997 before reviewing it again, even though the 1994 review had failed to reach consensus on ways to promote its further development. In the interim and beyond the 1997 review, efforts to refine the UNROCA must turn elsewhere, with the potential for regional developments holding the most promise—as in South-East Asia.

Second, South-East Asia is a relatively small region, which makes it easier to develop multilateral approaches to arms trade and defence-related transparency mechanisms. The size and scale of the group also mean that arms acquisitions, holdings and domestic production are relatively small, which will make information-sharing and -monitoring efforts relatively easier.

Third, throughout the nearly 30-year history of the Association of South-East Asian Nations (ASEAN)[8] most countries of South-East

[7] The 7 reporting categories of the UNROCA—battle tanks, armoured combat vehicles, large-calibre artillery, combat aircraft, attack helicopters, warships, and missiles and missile launchers—are fairly broad. In theory, then, an aircraft-carrier would belong in the same category as a small attack craft; and both would be represented simply as a number under 'warships' with no description of their obvious differences. Moreover, with an emphasis on land-based systems, the categories are probably less appropriate for the prevailingly maritime and archipelagic environment in South-East Asia.

[8] As of 1 Jan. 1997, the 7 members of ASEAN were: Brunei, Indonesia, Malaysia, the Philippines, Singapore, Thailand and Viet Nam. Cambodia, Laos and Myanmar are expected to join ASEAN in the near future.

Asia have developed substantial experience in multilateral approaches to diplomatic problem-solving. To put it another way, an official culture of cooperation and openness at the regional level already exists, often known as the 'ASEAN process' or 'ASEAN way', a form of cooperative multilateralism that is noticeably absent elsewhere in the Asia–Pacific region and throughout most of the world. The ASEAN way will present a number of obstacles to developing arms- and defence-related transparency mechanisms in South-East Asia. At the same time, however, its flexibility, informality and consensus-building aspects have proved amenable in the past to concepts of comprehensive security and CBMs.[9]

ASEAN has played a leading role in efforts to establish and sustain other cooperative, multilateral, security-enhancing organizations such as the ASEAN Post-Ministerial Meetings and the ASEAN Regional Forum (ARF).[10] The ARF has explicitly expressed its support for its members to participate in formal and informal arms- and defence-related transparency measures. In particular, the ARF Concept Paper, issued in 1995, includes a list of such CBMs and proposals to be considered and possibly implemented by ARF participants. These include participation in the UNROCA, publication of defence White Papers, 'exploration of a Regional Arms Register', and other such measures.[11]

In addition, the 'track-two process' of semi- and unofficial security-related dialogue among academic experts and officials in South-East Asia is well established and offers a widely respected and considerable source of support and direction to discussions at the official level. The fundamental norms and mechanisms for multilateral discussions are thus already in place and provide a good basis on which

[9] See also chapter 4 in this volume.

[10] The ARF was founded in July 1993 during the ASEAN Post-Ministerial Meeting in Singapore and the first formal meeting of the group was held in Bangkok in July 1994. Subsequent meetings have been held annually, supplemented by intersessional meetings at the working level. The ARF was formed as the largest multilateral body in the Asia–Pacific region dedicated to addressing security issues at the official level. Among other declarations, the ARF has formally endorsed participation of its members in the UNROCA and encouraged its membership to submit, on a voluntary basis, annual statements of defence policy. As of 1 Jan. 1997, the members of ARF were: Australia, Brunei, Cambodia, Canada, China, the European Union, India, Indonesia, Japan, South Korea, Laos, Malaysia, Myanmar, New Zealand, Papua New Guinea, the Philippines, Russia, Singapore, Thailand, the United States and Viet Nam.

[11] ASEAN, The ASEAN Regional Forum: A Concept Paper, attached to the 'Chairman's statement at the Second ASEAN Regional Forum, (ARF), Aug. 1995, Bandar Seri Begawan (Brunei)'.

to explore and advance appropriate approaches to arms trade and defence-related transparency in South-East Asia.

Fourth, the region is currently embarked on a substantial arms modernization drive which is unfolding amid continuing unresolved differences and security problems and against a background of the development of more externally oriented and contingency-driven security and arms acquisition policies. Under these conditions arms build-ups, unless properly handled, could result in unnecessary tensions, suspicions and instabilities. Exploration and possible implementation of arms-related transparency approaches seem to be warranted as a means to ease the uncertainties presented by the current arms modernization process in South-East Asia.

Other approaches tend to focus on transparency in the Asia–Pacific region as a whole, particularly among those countries involved in the ARF. However, as with the development of other multilateral security forums in the Asia–Pacific region, it will be the South-East Asian nations and particularly the members of ASEAN which have the strongest influence over the development of arms- and defence-related transparency mechanisms in the region. The size, diversity and relative inexperience of the ARF will likely slow progress at the official level on arms- and defence-related transparency measures within the ARF, and lingering tensions and suspicions such as exist particularly among the northern members of the ARF—including great-power rivalries, territorial disputes and other difficulties—do not exist to the same degree in South-East Asia.

Reflecting on the realities of the ARF and recognizing ASEAN's already impressive accomplishments of multilateralism and leadership, it makes more sense to explore the possibilities for progress among South-East Asian nations first and then determine the suitability of transparency measures on a broader scale.

III. Concepts, conditions and new approaches

With these principles and definitions in mind, the chapters which follow lay out a foundation upon which discussions on arms, transparency and security might build in the years ahead. The approach taken by most authors in this volume seeks to provide experts and policy makers with a better understanding of the prevailing concepts of, conditions for and possible approaches to questions of arms, transparency and security in South-East Asia.

Chapter 2 by Laurance sets the conceptual context within which arms, transparency and security issues should be discussed. It illustrates that if arms- and defence-related transparency mechanisms are to develop they must do so at the regional level. Laurance details the five principal concepts or components which should accompany any attempt to construct a viable mechanism aimed at promoting arms- and defence-related transparency and argues why these concepts would be most effective at regional level.

The approach to arms-related transparency developed by Laurance remains at a mostly conceptual stage and cannot be readily implemented in South-East Asia today, but it will be precisely these conceptual issues which need to be considered more seriously as South-East Asian experts and policy makers move forward in their debate on arms, transparency and security in the region. In recognizing this point, Laurance offers a number of initial, practical steps which might be taken in the region to strengthen the process of arms- and defence-related transparency.

Moving from the conceptual to the actual, the next three chapters present current and likely future strategic and political conditions in South-East Asia, especially as they relate to the possible development of arms and defence-related information-sharing and transparency measures. In chapter 3 Swinnerton sets out the many security-related concerns which exist in the region and explains how these concerns often serve to justify arms acquisitions. At the same time, he notes the several positive developments within the strategic environment which help to build confidence and trust within the region.

In chapter 4 Mak focuses on explaining the pros and cons of the ASEAN way for the development of arms and defence-related transparency. He proposes a number of ASEAN-specific transparency approaches and argues that the changing nature of the security environment requires ASEAN to adapt its approaches to strengthen CBMs, particularly those related to arms and defence issues. In chapter 5 Acharya builds on Mak's contribution by presenting a comprehensive survey of past, current and likely future defence cooperation activities among South-East Asian nations. While the record is impressive, Acharya cautions that more ambitious proposals for multilateral security-related confidence building—including defence-related transparency measures—will face considerable constraints and must be developed patiently step by step.

The three final chapters look ahead, provide examples of certain approaches to transparency and suggest ways in which they might be adapted for use in South-East Asia. In chapter 6 Gill seeks to stimulate and give definition to a more active debate on what constitutes legitimate as opposed to unwarranted military development in the region. In doing so he shows that broad areas of consensus already exist on this question in South-East Asia and spells out several specific definitions and models which could be utilized as the region develops its own approach to transparency.

Following Gill, Choi and Panitan in chapter 7 take up the value of defence White Papers as a form of transparency, set out a number of standards by which defence White Papers might be evaluated, and describe their development in the Asia–Pacific region, including a special case study on the Thai defence White Paper. They conclude by suggesting a number of particularly relevant recommendations for the future development of defence White Papers in the region. Chapter 8 by Wezeman describes the pitfalls and benefits of the development of open-source arms trade registers such as the one maintained by SIPRI. For any person or institution contemplating the establishment of either an official or an unofficial arms register, this chapter provides extensive insights.

At the conclusion of the volume, Wezeman and the SIPRI Arms Transfers Project offer a highly detailed de facto register of arms imports and licensed arms production for South-East Asia covering the period 1975–96. Based on the SIPRI arms transfers database, this appendix provides an extensive, authoritative and unique data set which will prove useful to policy makers, security analysts, journalists and other observers concerned with arms, transparency and security in the region.

Taken together, the work offered in this volume seeks to make a modest but meaningful contribution to the ongoing debate over the development of openness and transparency in defence affairs as an approach to confidence building in South-East Asia. The contributions are not intended to constrain or strictly define this debate. Rather, they hope to offer some of the analytical, empirical and practical tools necessary for the debate to expand and progress in ways which will enhance security and prosperity in South-East Asia.

2. A conceptual framework for arms trade transparency in South-East Asia

Edward J. Laurance

I. Introduction

The two UN expert groups that reviewed the United Nations Register of Conventional Arms (UNROCA) reached consensus on two points. First, theory regarding registers is in the nascent stage of development and no generally agreed theory exists. Second, if such theories are to develop, they should do so at the regional level. Drawing on the experience of developing the UNROCA, this chapter puts forward a theoretical framework to guide the work of those inside and outside government who are exploring the development of arms-related transparency and information exchange mechanisms at the regional level.

Section II of this chapter establishes a five-point conceptual framework outlining how a transparency instrument such as a register can theoretically prevent arms build-ups from leading to conflict. Section III then presents a set of factors which will determine the likelihood of success for such a regional register—factors which must be evaluated and developed by actors and analysts in the South-East Asian region. These criteria lead to section IV and a set of next steps which might be employed to guide the development of a transparency mechanism in South-East Asia.

II. Theoretical framework

The term 'register' implies more than the mere compilation of militarily relevant data. In this chapter and throughout the volume the term is used to represent an all-encompassing mechanism constructed to prevent the excessive and destabilizing accumulation of conventional arms. Five components are necessary for an arms register to function effectively (see figure 2.1).

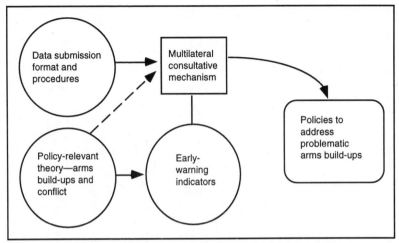

Figure 2.1. Theoretical framework for an arms register as a confidence-building measure

Component one: multilateral data submission

Using transparency as the basis for arms control is very different from the approaches that were used during the cold war. For most of this period the only arms control that existed, for example in dealing with the negative consequences of the arms trade, was unilateral. Supplier states made their own assessments as to what exports would be destabilizing and controlled them at the national level.[1] Those multilateral attempts at conventional arms control in the cold war (for instance, the US–Soviet Conventional Arms Transfer Talks (CATT), the Coordinating Committee on Multilateral Export Controls (COCOM) and the Missile Technology Control Regime (MTCR)) were mainly attempts by suppliers to prevent acquisitions from occurring in the first place.

Both the unilateral and the multilateral approach to arms control are illustrated in the part of the basic model (figure 2.2) depicted by box A. The arms control effort occurs before the integration of the armaments into the national arsenal and therefore before the actual

[1] For a discussion of the dominance of unilateral over multilateral approaches to controlling the international arms trade during the cold war, see Laurance, E. J., 'Reducing the negative consequences of arms transfers through unilateral arms control', ed. B. Ramberg, *Arms Control Without Negotiation: From the Cold War to the New World Order* (Lynne Rienner Publishers: Boulder, Colo., 1993), pp. 175–98.

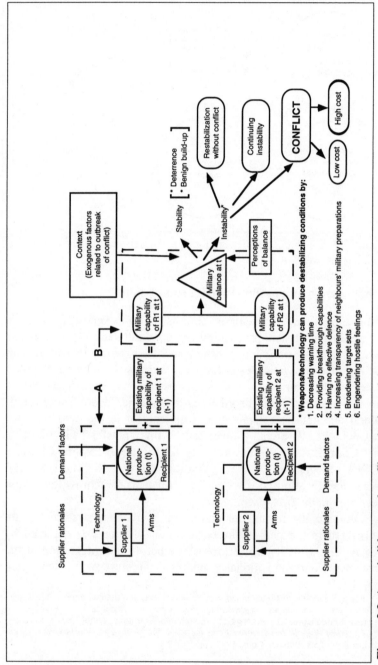

Figure 2.2. Arms build-ups and conflict: a basic model

addition of a military capability that could lead to a destabilizing military balance. Any decision to prevent or limit such transfers, especially if they have significant economic implications, is difficult to reach. Moreover, in the post-cold war era global and domestic markets for armaments have shrunk and there is no clear ideological threat, so that willingness to limit or regulate the arms trade is further diminished. As a result both the unilateral and the multilateral models have shown themselves to be ineffective, which has led to the development of a third approach, that of transparency.

The transparency approach is fundamentally different from the unilateral and multilateral models. First, it is a confidence-building and cooperative effort, in contrast to unilateral or most multilateral approaches which are based on supply-side export denial. Negotiated, cooperative transparency is an effort to reduce mistrust, misperception and miscalculation of another country's intentions in the field of military security and, if possible, to build partnership, trust and norms as to legitimate needs and unwarranted development of military capacity.

Second, the operating principle of this model is that negative effects of arms build-ups cannot be determined until a military balance is developed (or is developing) in the first place. This means that any arms control efforts will necessarily occur later in the arms build-up pattern depicted in the basic model—the area marked by box B in figure 2.2. It also means that any mechanism designed to deal with these build-ups must take into account the level at which a state begins its build-up (i.e., its current holdings) and what it acquires in addition through national production as well as imports. It is important that arms-related transparency and information exchange mechanisms develop data which will allow the assessment of any military balance that evolves. Further, states can then use these data to correct any misperceptions that may arise and thereby prevent arms build-ups from leading to conflict.

This is not to say that those suppliers who did exercise restraint during the cold war (as most did) did not contribute to the knowledge of when arms acquisitions can be excessive or destabilizing,[2] but their

[2] For example, the USA held back from selling F-16 fighter aircraft to South Korea during the late 1970s for fear that North Korea would go back to its patron, the USSR, for the comparable MiG-23, the end result being a higher level of military capability on the peninsula and renewed strategic access for the USSR. There were many examples of supplier states refusing to sell arms to countries engaged in civil war for fear of adding fuel to a raging fire.

action was typically unilateral: no multilateral institutions were involved and the lessons were not internationalized. The 1991 Persian Gulf War changed all this. For the first time the international community talked in terms of an excessive and destabilizing accumulation of conventional arms.

In the case of the UNROCA, transparency is achieved when member states voluntarily submit militarily relevant data to a multilateral institution charged with data storage and dissemination. This component consists of the form on which states submit data and the instructions developed to guide these submissions. The UN Centre for Disarmament Affairs (UNCDA) provides technical advice to states regarding these procedures and stores and disseminates the data, although degrees of detail on the submissions will vary

The architects of the UNROCA hurried through the development of data structure. In the end they suggested seven categories of major weapon systems, providing a brief definition for each. The consensus among participants at the time was that the first five categories would closely follow the five categories of the 1990 Treaty on Conventional Armed Forces in Europe (CFE Treaty): tanks, armoured personnel carriers (APCs), long-range artillery, combat aircraft and attack helicopters. The final two categories, combat ships and missiles and missile launchers, were added to reflect the experience of the Persian Gulf War.

The states developing the UNROCA were divided as to whether militarily relevant data should include procurement through national production and military holdings as well as exports and imports. They could only agree on exports and imports and postponed the decision on the other two categories of data. One expert group was charged with developing a form which could be easily filled in by member states. The debates which raged over this seemingly straightforward task indicate that constructing even this component of the transparency mechanism at the regional level will not be simple.

Throughout the process it was known that the procedural component of the register would have shortcomings, mainly because a form and set of submission procedures had to be developed which covered all member states. This resulted in many states viewing the register as an irrelevant exercise, since the categories of equipment were irrelevant in their region. Security concerns also vary from region to region. While the seven UN categories may be pertinent to South-East

Asia, debates there on developing appropriate weapon categories for transparency mechanisms need to consider the region's specific security environment.

Component two: linking arms build-ups to instability and conflict

Before devising policies for controlling the negative effects of arms build-ups through arms control and other approaches, analysts must first deal with the critical issue of the link between arms build-ups and conflict.[3] Figure 2.2 shows a model of how arms imports and/or indigenous production can lead to destabilization and eventually armed conflict. For the purposes of this discussion it is assumed that the two countries concerned are adjacent developing countries.

Arms build-ups are the result of policy decisions by both arms suppliers and recipients. Supplier states use a variety of military, political and economic rationales for exporting armaments. Similar factors in recipient states lead to their acquisition of armaments. Some recipient states acquire additional armaments through indigenous production. The result, as depicted in figure 2.2, is that at any given time the military capabilities of two states are a function of acquired armaments modified by both force multipliers (e.g., command and control capabilities) and factors such as personnel, maintenance and doctrine, which can sometimes result in capability lower than appears to be represented by the armaments themselves.[4]

If the analyst is to assess stability in military relationships (which is a necessary part of a transparency regime worthy of the name) even larger analytical tasks remain: determining when an arms build-up is 'excessive and destabilizing'; when a particular type of weapon system is destabilizing; and when the deployment of particular types of weapon in a particular manner enhances the likelihood of conflict. As noted in the diagram, Mussington and Sislin have identified at least six characteristics of military acquisitions, build-ups and subsequent balances which increase the likelihood of producing destabilizing conditions.[5] The arms control task is nothing less than the develop-

---

[3] For an in-depth analysis, see Pearson, F. S. and Brzoska, M., *Arms and Warfare: Escalation, Deescalation, Negotiation* (University of South Carolina Press: Columbia, S.C., 1994).

[4] For a complete discussion of these modifiers, see Laurance, E. J., *The International Arms Trade* (Lexington Books: New York, 1992), pp. 16–40.

[5] Specifically, destabilization and conflict are more likely when armaments and equipment are acquired which by their intrinsic nature lead to any of the following: decreased warning

ment of multilateral early-warning indicators and a consultative mechanism which can assess when these indicators point to conflict.

Complicating this analytical task is the reality that military balances are always part of a larger economic and political context. A set of objective contextual factors determines how the military balance will contribute to destabilization and conflict, if at all. These factors comprise the well-known set of established 'causes of war', which in most cases will explain conflict more completely than the military balance. The perceptions of the parties involved are also included in determining a military balance. History is full of examples of states which have launched pre-emptive attacks having misperceived an adversary's capabilities or intentions. Similarly, miscalculations of military capabilities and balances have allowed aggressor states to start wars.

During the cold war with its focus on nuclear weapons there was some consensus as to how nuclear weapon build-ups were linked to war. The fear of first-strike capability was based not only on presumed hostile intentions but also on military capabilities designed for a first strike. Fortunately for mankind, no empirical data were ever generated to test these propositions. In the case of regional conflict with conventional weapons, however, the link is much more ambiguous.

Focusing on this link between arms build-ups and conflict also reveals other realities that have (or should have) a major effect on arms control approaches. First, there are no international legal instruments which control either the production of or the trade in conventional weapons as there are with weapons of mass destruction. The laws that govern conventional arms build-ups are national in scope, with the exception of Articles 2(4) and 51 of the UN Charter, which establish that no state may interfere in the affairs of another and that every state has a right to defend itself. With the possible exception of the CFE Treaty, there is no internationally agreed legal limit to the level at which a state can be armed with conventional weapons. Second, in most cases arms build-ups do not lead to conflict, since they may create stability through mutual deterrence or exist in a political context where little reason for armed conflict exists, making arms build-ups and subsequent balances benign. (See the range of out-

time; provision of breakthrough capabilities; no effective defence against the weapon; one side gaining insight into the other side's military preparations; a broadening of target sets; and the engendering of hostile feelings. Mussington, D. and Sislin, J., 'Defining destabilizing arms acquisitions', *Jane's Intelligence Review*, vol. 17, no. 2 (Feb. 1995), pp. 88–90.

comes ·depicted in figure 2.2.) The dilemma for both national and international policy makers is to develop indicators to assist in determining when and how arms build-ups may lead to the outbreak of armed conflict.

Component three: early-warning indicators

Assuming that outside experts, states or multilateral institutions begin to deal with the policy-relevant theory discussed above, this theory must eventually lead to a set of concrete indicators that would alert the members of a regional arms-related transparency mechanism to the fact that a troublesome build-up is occurring. The indicators developed by Mussington and Sislin are an example. These indicators should be extensive enough to provide a comprehensive context in which to interpret a given acquisition. Very few acquisitions can be labelled 'offensive' or 'defensive' at face value. Nevertheless a set of indicators can be devised which can assist member states in evaluating the nature of a given acquisition. This is discussed further in chapter 6 in this volume. Moreover, military capability is more than just an inventory of end items: the acquisition of major items such as main battle tanks, missile boats or combat aircraft can be more or less destabilizing depending on maintenance capability, ammunition and spare parts which may accompany the acquisition. It is highly unlikely that the data produced by member states will ever take into account all these factors. Rather, they will need to be addressed as part of the deliberations of a consultative mechanism.

At present, discussions aimed at developing such early-warning indicators are at a relatively early stage, both globally and in South-East Asia. However, official statements as well as track-two activities in South-East Asia suggest that such discussions may be moving forward.[6]

---

[6] Syed Hamid Albar, Defence Minister of Malaysia, quoted in 'Malaysia calls for measures to bar regional arms race', *International Herald Tribune*, 7 Feb. 1996, p. 4; Babbage, R., 'Enhancing national military capabilities in the Asia Pacific region: legitimate needs versus unwarranted development', Paper presented at the ASEAN–ISIS Asia–Pacific Roundtable, Kuala Lumpur, 5–8 June 1995; and Gill, B., 'Enhancing national military capabilities in the Asia Pacific region: legitimate needs versus unwarranted development', Paper presented at the ASEAN–ISIS Asia–Pacific Roundtable, Kuala Lumpur, 5–8 June 1995.

Component four: a multilateral consultative mechanism

Arms trade transparency approaches to security will depend on a multilateral institution where data, policy-relevant theory and early-warning indicators can be addressed. The story of the UNROCA is instructive. At first glance the 1990 Iraqi invasion of Kuwait seemed to prod the global system into adopting a confidence-building mechanism which requested that states publicly register their exports and imports in the seven major categories of armaments. Some countries, such as Egypt, India and Pakistan, released such information despite difficult security situations on their borders, fully expecting the development of a serious, functional international consultative mechanism that would allow prudent and timely discussion of the data that had been made transparent. When it became clear that the major arms supplier states did not want such a mechanism, their zeal for the UNROCA dropped. No serious analysis was done on this aspect of its implementation, despite the fact that several existing institutions—the UNCDA, the UN Disarmament Commission and the First Committee of the UN General Assembly—could have served in this role.

Central to the development of a confidence-building mechanism is the ability to answer questions that arise as a result of information exchanges. An example from the UNROCA illustrates this need. One of the rationales for the UNROCA was the prevention of 'excessive and destabilizing' accumulations of conventional arms, but who or which body will determine what is excessive and destabilizing? The Conference on Disarmament was given the task of coming up with a general definition of this condition and, not unexpectedly, failed.

A consultative mechanism which goes beyond traditional diplomacy—an established body which would meet regularly to review the data, theory and early-warning indicators—appears to be necessary. The functions of such a mechanism would be, first, to lower the political and economic costs of addressing excessive and destabilizing arms build-ups, particularly if such a process is to be part of the UN system. A way has to be found to make the questioning of build-ups not always a matter of high politics but rather a part of confidence building characterized by low politics. Second, a consultative mechanism could also define 'excessive and destabilizing' by developing a set of parameters used by non-governmental experts to render objective assessments of military balances. Gradually, this body of experts could gain the confidence of states concerned. It would have to ensure that all parties to any issue raised were participants. In sum, it must be a setting for raising issues and building confidence on issues related to arms trade and acquisition concerns.

Component five: policies to address arms build-ups

It is clear that, once a build-up has been identified as excessive or destabilizing by the multilateral consultative mechanism, policies must be developed and executed to deal with it. For example, the Conference on Security and Co-operation in Europe (CSCE) concluded that the end of the cold war meant that the arsenals which existed in Europe were no longer needed at those levels. The result was the CFE Treaty, which obligated the member states to build down to agreed levels. For a regional arms-related transparency arrangement to work effectively, a full range of policy tools should be available. These might include cooperative defence efforts to reduce the cost of national defence for the partner states, arms embargoes, development credits for disarmament and agreements as to rules of engagement. A wide range of policy tools will allow member states flexibly to apply measures to address build-ups which are suited to specific contexts and situations.

III. Regional approaches to arms trade transparency

At the global level the UNROCA has only partly developed according to the model in figure 2.2. There are some problems with data submission, although that component is fairly well developed. Components two and three have not evolved, mainly because of the absence of component four, a multilateral consultative mechanism which could critically review the data produced by the member states for the UNROCA. In the absence of any deliberation on arms build-ups, nothing has been done in the way of identifying or dealing with such build-ups.

In some respects, the failure of a meaningful consultative mechanism to develop at the global level is understandable. Such a global mechanism may well have some value as an arms control mechanism in the sense that it would promote the sharing not only of information but also of expertise in assessing military balances. In the final analysis, the presence of excessive and destabilizing accumulations of conventional arms is best determined at the regional level.

The regionalization of the UNROCA has been a part of the exercise from the start. Paragraph 17 of UN Resolution 46/36L (9 December 1991) establishing the UNROCA 'calls upon all Member States to cooperate at a regional and subregional level, taking fully into account the specific conditions prevailing in the region or subregion, with a view to enhancing and coordinating international efforts aimed at increased openness and transparency in armaments'. In an address to the UN Advisory Board on Disarmament Matters, the UN Secretary-General supported this approach: 'Regional registers should now be the next step. They have the advantage of allowing the categories of weapons to be registered to reflect the security concerns felt in the region'.[7]

The 1994 Group of Experts report put great emphasis on regionalization as the next step for the UNROCA: 'In order to promote wider participation in the Register, a regional approach may be beneficial . . . the group took note of relevant initiatives of some regional organizations or forums'. The report added that 'regional and subregional efforts should be encouraged. They may pave the way for a higher degree of openness, confidence and transparency in the region' and 'could address the possible regional security concerns relating to participation in the Register'.[8]

Benefits of the regional approach

Data submission in the first years of the UNROCA varied widely by region, providing further evidence that regionalization of the arms transparency process may well bring immediate dividends. For example, interviews with representatives of several African states, where the participation rate was very low, indicated that this was largely due to a lack of relevance: the seven categories of armaments, mainly sophisticated and expensive items found in industrialized states, are not the arms of concern for many African states. Presumably regional mechanisms could be designed to deal with those

[7] United Nations, Address of the Secretary-General to the Advisory Board on Disarmament Matters, UN document SG/SM/94/3, 12 Jan. 1994.

[8] United Nations, Report on the continuing operation of the United Nations Register of Conventional Arms and its further development, UN document A/49/316, 22 Sep. 1994, paras 23, 38, 39.

weapons accumulated in the region. Regional variants could also take into account factors such as the culture of transparency and the civil–military relationship, which vary significantly from region to region.

It is no accident that where regional organizations exist regional approaches to transparency are seeing some progress. For example, the Organization for Security and Co-operation in Europe (OSCE)[9] has continued to take the lead in transparency and consultative mechanisms. In the developing world, the Organization of American States (OAS) recently formed a Permanent Council on Cooperation for Hemispheric Security. At its June 1995 meeting it adopted a resolution urging all members to participate fully in the UNROCA, supply the UN with information on their defence spending regularly, exchange UNROCA data between member states, and at the regional level 'regularly engage in discussions, consultations, and exchanges of data supplied to the UN Register and data on national policies, laws, and administrative procedures governing arms transfers and defense spending'.[10]

In South-East Asia the ARF has directly addressed this issue. At its first summit meeting, held in Bangkok in July 1994, all members agreed to a resolution calling for 'the eventual participation of all ARF countries in the Register'.[11] In the second ARF meeting, held in Brunei in 1995, the ministers present agreed 'to take note of the increased participation in the UN Conventional Arms Register since the first ARF and encourage those not yet participating to soon do so'.[12]

Not only is the link between arms build-ups and destabilization or conflict critical for understanding arms control; it also varies significantly from one region to another. Most recently this can be seen in assessments of the 'arms race' in East Asia. States in the region have been quick to respond with a host of explanations—such as modernization and general economic well-being—rather than offensive threats or security problems. Different regions are likely to have different security environments and perceptions. A regional transparency approach with the associated consultative mechanisms would be more

---

[9] Formerly the CSCE.

[10] Organization of American States, Report of the Permanent Council on Cooperation for Hemispheric Security, Washington, DC, 5 June 1995, p. 6.

[11] 'Chairman's statement of the First ASEAN Regional Forum', 25 July 1994, p. 3.

[12] Quoted from 'Chairman's statement of the Second ASEAN Regional Forum (ARF), Aug. 1995, Bandar Seri Begawan', provided to the Northeast Asia Peace and Security Network by the Pacific Forum CSIS, Honolulu.

likely to yield accurate explanations of acquisition behaviour and military developments than a universal register or a global approach.

Value of the global register for regional variants

A regional transparency approach, however, should not ignore the value of a global register. First, the UNROCA establishes some basic global norms such as transparency and the need to avoid or prevent destabilizing accumulations of conventional arms. Second, it is an incubator for techniques and procedures that might be utilized or enhanced at the regional level. Third, an international institution, the UNCDA, exists and operates as part of the UNROCA machinery. Fourth, such a global institution also allows regional actors to interact multilaterally with non-regional actors, especially arms exporters. Finally, the UNROCA as a global confidence-building mechanism has brought together states which normally dealt with this issue only through rhetoric. This is especially apparent in the operation of the two expert groups where states were forced to go beyond verbal charges and counter-charges and engage in the responsible negotiation of a text on the operation and expansion of the UNROCA.[13]

IV. Conclusions: the next steps

The time seems ripe for regions such as South-East Asia to consider seriously expanding on the idea of using transparency in armaments as the basis for confidence building and the prevention of destabilizing arms build-ups. The UNROCA has been a start in this direction but for a variety of reasons its development has stalled at the level of providing transparent data on arms exports and imports.

It is critical that all the components described here are addressed when crafting an arms-related transparency approach. For example,

---

[13] For additional analysis of regional registers, see Chalmers, M., 'Openness and security policy in South-East Asia', *Survival,* vol. 38, no. 3 (1996), pp. 82–98; Cossa, R. A. (ed.), *Promoting Regional Transparency: Defense Policy Papers and the United Nations Register of Conventional Arms* (Pacific Forum CSIS: Honolulu, July 1996); Chalmers, M. and Greene, O., 'The United Nations Register of Conventional Arms and the Asia–Pacific region', eds M. Chalmers and O. Greene, *The United Nations and the Asia–Pacific* (Department of Peace Studies, University of Bradford: Bradford, 1994), pp. 129–54; and DiChiaro, J., 'The UN Register in a regional context: basic concepts', eds M. Chalmers *et al.*, *Developing the UN Register of Conventional Arms* (Department of Peace Studies, University of Bradford: Bradford, 1994), pp. 271–80.

should South-East Asia develop a data submission scheme, member states might only interpret the data on their own without the benefit of a multilateral consultative mechanism where they could explain and put into context acquisitions which on the surface are perceived as destabilizing. Similarly, through a consultative process member states could define what 'destabilizing' means in their regional context and develop measures to address such acquisitions. The provision of data alone could increase misperceptions and detract from the goal of increasing security in the region.

The following suggestions are steps which might help develop transparency in the arms trade as a confidence-building measure in South-East Asia.

First, the major supplier states, or preferably the UN, should engage in activities which bolster the capacity of developing states to report data, assess military balances and build multilateral institutions which address the linkage between arms and conflict. In South-East Asia, as elsewhere, part of the reason for scepticism about new transparency initiatives is simply the lack of staff resources and information.

Second, the process requires more research and discussion at the regional and global level on how a consultative mechanism designed to process arms acquisition data would actually prevent excessive and destabilizing accumulations of conventional arms.

Third, more effort is needed to encourage greater understanding of and participation in the register process. For example, individual states should be encouraged to meet with the UNCDA before submitting their annual data to offer and receive technical advice, if nothing else. These visits could also be used to learn more about the actual operation of databases, reporting schedules and other matters related to the UNROCA. A group such as the ARF, which has committed itself to participation, could convene a workshop of the persons responsible for submissions built around the UNCDA 'how-to' manual on the UNROCA.[14] Not only could such a meeting handle basics and frequently asked questions; it could also discuss the experience of the first several years of the UNROCA's existence regarding discrepancies and mismatches. Organizations which publish public-source military information—such as Jane's Information Group or SIPRI—could be encouraged to make presentations which explain how the

[14] United Nations Centre for Disarmament Affairs, *Register of Convnetional Arms: Information Booklet* (UN: New York, N.Y., 1993).

arms trade is to a large degree already transparent. At a minimum participants would see that a significant amount of information is already available, which might serve to break down some of the barriers to openness. At the time of writing the UNCDA had organized and conducted six such regional meetings on the UNROCA with positive results, but none in South-East Asia.

Fourth, either in conjunction with the above-mentioned workshop or separately, the next step should be an assessment of which conditions exist in South-East Asia that would support the development of confidence-building measures such as arms trade transparency, considering the key factors developed above. Such an assessment should highlight those factors which need further development before an all-out effort is made to develop a regional arms trade transparency mechanism.

Finally, much research needs to be done on the link between arms build-ups and armed conflict. The cases where build-ups have led to armed conflict are in the minority but are disastrous when they occur. It is, however, just as important to document and model those cases where arms build-ups have not led to conflict. Without such knowledge, we are left with the argument that all weapons are destabilizing and must be eliminated. Policy makers and analysts must get beyond disarmament to arms control. For those concerned with arms trade transparency and security in South-East Asia, the framework, concepts and suggestions presented here are offered as a foundation on which such an approach might be crafted.

3. The strategic environment and arms acquisitions in South-East Asia

Russ Swinnerton

I. Introduction

The military and security situation in South-East Asia is viewed with interest and some concern both within and outside South-East Asia. Of particular interest, arms acquisitions in South-East Asia are variously characterized as lying somewhere between the extremes of benign modernization and a destabilizing arms race, depending on the commentator's proximity and viewpoint. Even within the region views vary. Perceptions of the regional security environment in South-East Asia with the end of the cold war fall similarly between extremes: on the one hand a view of a robust, economically pragmatic world where market forces will settle any differences, and on the other the idea of a dangerously unstable and uncertain power vacuum.

Despite the end of the cold war, the security imperatives in the region are the same as they have always been—regional rivalries (including disputed sovereignty), external power interests and trade issues. In an effort to better understand this situation and its effect on transparency and confidence-building mechanisms in the region, this chapter presents the defining geo-strategic features of the region with a particular focus on maritime concerns and considers their role in stimulating current South-East Asian arms acquisitions before briefly taking stock of developments in transparency and trust building.

II. Defining features

Regional rivalries and territorial disputes

The concept of South-East Asia as a discrete region began to gain currency after World War II.[1] Before that, 9 of the 10 countries recognized today as belonging to the region (the 7 members of ASEAN,

---

[1] Thayer, C. A., 'Asia Pacific security: problems and prospects: an Australian perspective', Paper presented at Malaysian Strategic Research Centre/Australian Defence Studies Centre Seminar, Kuala Lumpur, 27 Sep. 1995.

Table 3.1. Disputed maritime claims and boundaries in South-East Asia

---

Competing claims to the Paracel Islands (Xisha Quandao or Quan Doa Hoang Sa) in the South China Sea, contested by China and Viet Nam

Competing claims to the Spratly Islands in the South China Sea, contested by China, Viet Nam, Brunei, Malaysia, Taiwan and the Philippines

Boundary dispute between Indonesia and Viet Nam on their demarcation line on the continental shelf in the South China Sea, near Natuna Island

Boundary dispute between China and Viet Nam on their demarcation line on the continental shelf in the Gulf of Tonkin

Boundary dispute between Malaysia and Viet Nam on their offshore demarcation line

Dispute between Malaysia and Singapore over ownership of the island of Pulau Batu Putih (Pedra Branca or Horsburgh Light), some 55 km east of Singapore in the Straits of Johore

Competing claims to the islands of Sipidan, Sebatik and Ligitan, in the Celebes Sea, some 35 km from Semporna in Sabah, contested by Indonesia and Malaysia

---

Source: Swinnerton, R. and Ball, D., *A Regional Regime for Maritime Surveillance, Safety and Information Exchange,* Working Paper no. 278 (Strategic and Defence Studies Centre, Australian National University: Canberra, Dec. 1993), appendix 1, table 1.

Cambodia, Laos and Myanmar) were parts of European empires. Only Thailand has never been a colony of a European power.

Developments in the region since the end of World War II have reflected the emergence of states from colonial status, the conclusion of their wars of ideology and their cooperative movement towards a sense of regional identity. The states themselves are still significantly different in character, religion, ideology, politics and philosophy, but the region's dynamism and post-colonial history also help to establish a broader sense of community.

In a region with such a complex history and range of cultures, a combined population of over 400 million and an even division of geographic area between sea and land it is not surprising that several points of contention exist—or that the region has devised means of dealing with problems (the 'ASEAN way'), stressing mutual respect, good-neighbourliness, consensus building and deferral of difficult issues to avoid open confrontation.[2] The new maritime environment following the entry into force of the UN Convention on the Law of the

---

[2] See chapter 4 in this volume.

Sea (UNCLOS) in November 1994 has reinforced the traditional concerns of an ASEAN largely made up of islands, archipelagos and peninsulas.[3] The particular territorial stress points are shown in table 3.1. Viet Nam features prominently and has a long history of negotiation with China over such issues. These disputes (and the dialogue with China) will now presumably be cast into an ASEAN context in a way that adds an interesting dynamic to Viet Nam's entry into ASEAN.

These sovereignty disputes in themselves may not cause armed conflict between South-East Asian countries, but their existence can exacerbate tensions arising over other difficulties. Supporters of the ASEAN way argue that minor irritants would never be a cause of war, whether or not the issue was combined with another territorial dispute. Nevertheless, neighbours inevitably view each other with occasional suspicion and keep their contingency planners preoccupied with the details of each other's strategies, capabilities and hardware:

While ASEAN member-states have been reticent about threats emanating to members from within the ASEAN organisation, the foreign and defence policies of the member-states, as well as the pattern of arms procurement, would tend to indicate that more often than not the enemy the ASEAN states are trying to overcome comes from within the organisation rather than without, even though this is never openly stated or identified.[4]

External interest and intervention

In the past, extra-regional countries' interests in South-East Asia turned on the same US–Soviet balance that preoccupied the world during the cold war. With an inward-looking former USSR no longer an active participant and the USA perceived to be disengaging, the security environment in the region is apparently less certain and less predictable. The alliances and interplay between China, the USSR and Viet Nam were clearly of key importance to the emergence and development of ASEAN; the conclusion of that ideological conflict and Viet Nam's entry into ASEAN are clear markers of the extent of the change that has occurred.

[3] Mack, A. and Ball, D., 'The military build-up in Asia–Pacific', *Pacific Review*, vol. 5, no. 3 (1992), p. 205.

[4] Singh, B., 'ASEAN's arms procurements: challenge of the security dilemma in the post-cold war era', *Comparative Strategy*, vol. 12 (1993), p. 217.

The emergence of China as an economic, political and strategic power (and potential superpower) has meant that China now preoccupies strategic analysis. This analysis of course includes the potential balance from other large players, principally the USA and Japan, but also including India and the Korean peninsula.

On the South-East Asian perception of US disengagement from the region:

The original cold war ideological and geopolitical rationales for United States forward presence and for American alliances in the region have lost most of their force. Not surprisingly, the prospect of continued long-term American commitment to the region seems increasingly questionable to some regional defence planners . . . [US withdrawal] is thus a 'worst-case' which regional defence planners *must* take seriously.[5]

Although the USA remains forward-deployed, the prospect of a less intensive presence, particularly at sea, encourages South-East Asian countries to increase their own capabilities at sea.

The interests of large external powers, however, continue to be felt in the region through a range of other factors, including: (*a*) the importance of sea lines of communication (SLOC) throughout the region, to China, Japan, the two Koreas, Taiwan and the US, and for continued regional economic development; (*b*) the interests of US and multinational oil companies prospecting in the Spratly Islands; and (*c*) the important markets for military hardware in South-East Asia (introducing more distant players, such as Germany, South Africa, Sweden and, in a new context, Russia).

The enduring feature marking the interest of external powers in the region, without the paradoxically stabilizing element of cold-war interest and attention, is the perception that their engagement renders the strategic security environment of the region less certain and less secure. The proximity of East Asia's main SLOC to the Spratly Islands, for instance, gives any potential disputes in this area extra-regional overtones: major trading powers will seek to ensure the freedom of the seas while remaining ostensibly neutral in local disputes. The complexity and importance of disputes over exclusive economic zones (EEZs) and seabed exploitation increase when conflicting exploration licences are granted by the parties to large multinational companies or countries outside the region. The zeal of foreign arms

---

[5] Mack and Ball (note 3), p. 204 (italics in original).

marketeers in satisfying (and, arguably, stimulating) demand for new military equipment also raises the kinds of questions that this study attempts to answer. In the face of such uncertainty, the countries of the region must take appropriate measures to acquire suitable capabilities for self-defence and protection of their vital interests.

Maritime economic issues

Tensions and regional rivalries do exist and are in the main managed by the ASEAN way of 'track-one' diplomacy. In addition to territorial disputes, the maritime context adds other sources of conflict, particularly in economic terms.

The entry into force of the UNCLOS has delivered two outcomes which are of relevance in this context. First, it has legitimized EEZ and continental shelf (seabed) claims out to 200 nautical miles, and, second, it has allowed recognition of archipelagic waters and associated transit regimes. The former factor adds emphasis to offshore economic issues, particularly oil and gas resources, and the latter adds a new dimension to the use of sea areas in the region for naval and commercial shipping.

Exclusive economic zones

Protection of EEZs takes on new importance with the UNCLOS, and the acquisition of maritime forces is the logical requirement and result. The armed forces of South-East Asia, with their historical preoccupation with counter-insurgency land wars, required urgent action to acquire the means effectively to control their EEZs. The categories of capability required include maritime surveillance, patrol and response, using ship, aircraft and land-based systems.

Disputed seabed EEZ boundaries are a potential source of friction, although joint development regimes are emerging which will assist in cooperative resolution. The key area of seabed/EEZ dispute is the Spratly Islands. The experience of the Philippines over Mischief Reef in early 1995 when China set down territorial markers on islets claimed by the Philippines has brought the Spratlys into sharp relief for all the ASEAN countries. Given China's superiority in conventional maritime arms compared to ASEAN, the Spratly claimants in ASEAN (Brunei, Malaysia, the Philippines and Viet Nam) will all need the ability to influence affairs at sea to the limit of their Spratlys claims, not for sea assertion or sea denial, but for 'sea credibility' or deterrence.

Fishing remains a continuing source of friction in the region, particularly between neighbours. Paramilitary and police action by South-East Asian maritime forces to counter illegal fishing occasionally results in loss of life. The realities of EEZ dominion combined with a diminishing supply and increasing demand will ensure that fishing remains a key point of concern between South-East Asian countries and a justification for the acquisition of maritime surveillance, patrol and response forces at the lower end of the capability spectrum.

Shipping

In general, regional shipping densities and the value and volumes of cargoes are all increasing. The combined gross domestic product (GDP) of the East Asian region is already around 70 per cent of those of the North Atlantic Free Trade Association (NAFTA) or Europe and increasing, and it is estimated that the region's GDP will overtake that of both North America and Europe between about 2010 and 2020. Imports into East Asia already have a combined value 20 per cent greater than those into North America.[6]

A significant part of this trade is seaborne: over 85 per cent of the world's trade travels in ships,[7] with trade volumes rapidly increasing in East Asia. Hong Kong reported a 30 per cent increase in containers handled in 1992 over 1991, with 7.97 million twenty-foot equivalent units (TEUs) handled, and a projected growth rate of 1 million TEUs per year.[8] This 1992 figure is almost double the volume handled in 1989. Hong Kong competes with Singapore as Asia's busiest container port, with Singapore achieving 7.56 million TEUs in 1992 at an annual growth rate of around 10 per cent.[9] Singapore is now poised to become the world's largest port (after coming a close second to Hong

---

[6] Sopiee, N., 'The new world order', *Confidence Building and Conflict Reduction in the Pacific* (ISIS Malaysia: Kuala Lumpur, 1993), pp. 21–22. East Asia is defined as Cambodia, China, Hong Kong, Japan, North Korea, South Korea, Laos, Myanmar, Taiwan, the Russian Far East and the ASEAN member states.

[7] van Fosen, A. B., *The International Political Economy of Pacific Island Flags of Convenience*, Australia–Asia Paper no. 66 (Griffith University: Brisbane, 1992), p. 5.

[8] 'HK world's busiest port', *Business Asia* (supplement to *The Australian*), 25 Aug. 1993, p. 24.

[9] 'Singapore chases shipping crown', *Business Asia* (supplement to *The Australian*), 8 Sep. 1993.

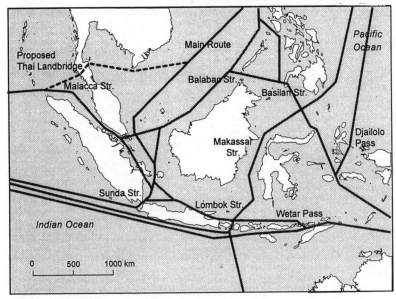

Figure 3.1. SLOCs in South-East Asia

Kong in 1993).[10] Kaohsiung, Pusan and Keelung have also registered strong growth in container volumes.[11] This traffic passes through the Indonesian Archipelago and island chains to the north, focused through several straits and areas of concentration (figure 3.1).

The maintenance of sea lines of communication is as much a responsibility for the owners of cargoes as it is for the coastal states. For imports and exports bound for or coming from ports within ASEAN, this responsibility is clearly ASEAN's, and it provides ample justification for the acquisition of appropriate maritime capabilities such as mine countermeasures and maritime air defence. States in the region which extract indirect advantage from shipping through providore services, bunkering and ship maintenance (Singapore, and increasingly Indonesia and Malaysia) will of course also be interested in maintaining the volume and benefit of the trade.

[10] 'Singapore poised to challenge Hong Kong as world's top container port', *Sarawak Tribune*, 20 June 1994, p. 15.

[11] Rimmer, P. and Dick, H., *Synthesising Australia: National Integration in a Dynamic Asia–Pacific Economy*, Papers of the Australian Transport Research Forum (Bureau of Transport and Communications Economics: Canberra, 1992), p. 295.

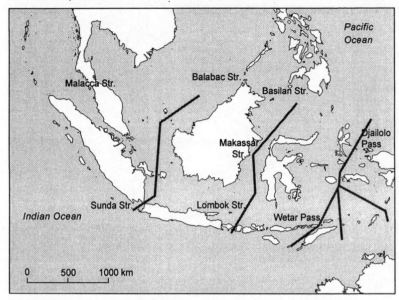

Figure 3.2. Indonesian proposals for SLOCs in South-East Asia

As mentioned above, the entry into force of the UNCLOS is likely to place further pressures on SLOC through the region. If Indonesia's proposal[12] to establish only three north/south and no east/west routes as archipelagic SLOCs were to come into effect, it would have a serious impact on shipping (figure 3.2). The region is fortunate to have a range of alternative routes, allowing the most economical route to be selected on the basis of weather, currents, ship size and cargo. To limit the selection of routes would impose additional costs which would have to be borne in higher commodity prices.

Sea robbery

The continued existence of piracy (more correctly termed sea robbery because it mainly occurs in territorial waters) is a challenge to shipping in the region. In commercial terms the damage done by piracy does not approach that done by other, less evocative, threats to

[12] Koeswanto, T. (Adm.), 'Indonesia's naval policy for the 1990s: territorial defence in the context of archipelagic doctrine', Paper presented at MIMA, Kuala Lumpur, 3 Dec. 1994. Adm. Koeswanto is Chief of Naval Staff of the Indonesian Navy.

cargoes such as fire, theft and weather, but piracy endangers crews' lives and there is a potential for environmental damage where ships are scuttled. Although piracy provides a useful justification for mounting cooperative patrols, very few pirates are caught (or arguably even deterred) by offshore patrols. When the frequency of piracy reaches a certain threshold, coastal states take unilateral action to resolve the problem using traditional policing methods. This threshold usually coincides with the point at which international cooperative operations are mounted (although it seems to be a fallacy to link international patrols with the reduction in pirate-like attacks).

Maritime fraud (including the use of disguised ship identities with bogus certificates of registry—phantom ships—to steal cargoes) is a potentially more significant problem. It is a particularly difficult type of cross-border crime to counter because of problems of jurisdiction and international cargo ownership.

Market factors and 'indefinables'

The end of the cold war is a factor in the increased availability of modern weapon systems and delivery platforms. Economic growth in the region also allows an increasing amount to be spent on arms and there is the additional dynamic of technology transfer. New state-of-the-art systems often bring with them a tail of technology which can be transferred into non-military applications, to the benefit of the recipient country. In addition, major suppliers—faced with post-cold war cutbacks in procurement orders—are seeking new markets in South-East Asia as their traditional customers reduce demand. Other factors are also at play in determining capability acquisition plans and priorities. Anecdotal information suggests that, as in the rest of the world, prestige, pecuniary interest and political factors have some bearing on weapon acquisitions: decisions are not always based on a rigorous evaluation of strategic imperatives and capability shortfalls.[13]

III. Justifying arms acquisitions in South-East Asia

The countries of the region have had (and some, to a limited extent, continue to have) insurgency difficulties within their boundaries. In the past, colonial oversight absolved them from responsibility for

---

[13] Suggested by Singh (note 4), p. 223.

external defence, which was in any case, before the UNCLOS, quite limited in a maritime sense. The states have progressed in their political and economic status, and are now financially, strategically and ideologically empowered to arm for conventional warfare.

The strategic basis for the build-up is not entirely clear—or, rather, not entirely public. The factors described above—regional rivalries, external country interests, trade issues and other factors—are all relevant to some extent. The imagery of Mischief Reef of course now features largely in contingency planning within the region. No South-East Asian country, including the Philippines, would wish to be in the same position of helplessness in the face of another Chinese initiative. In the case of the Philippines, the aftermath of Mischief Reef was a proposal for a $2 billion upgrade of the armed forces.[14] That is not to say that the countries of the region are arming to confront China, but they are ensuring an ability to influence activities in their proximate sea areas, achieving sea credibility or deterrence.

Several points will help to explain and clarify maritime arms acquisitions in the region. First, the trend is towards the acquisition of maritime weapon systems principally for a sea denial role. This includes maritime surveillance, patrol and response capabilities, and surface strike from surface and air platforms. Long-distance underway replenishment and logistic forces are not on the current acquisition lists, so power projection beyond the South China Sea is not possible. Some air-to-air refuelling capability is being acquired, but this is in the context of fairly limited fighter aircraft ranges and serves to improve time-on-task rather than increasing the radius of action.

Second, competition is clearly at play. Without challenging the general view that no arms race exists in the region, several commentators point to simultaneous acquisitions or 'competitive procurements', offering the example of air power procurement (fighter and strike aircraft) by Malaysia and Singapore since the late 1970s.[15] Similarly, the modernization of Singapore's maritime forces through the acquisition of submarine expertise and an old Swedish submarine has the potential to stimulate other 'modernizations' in the rest of South-East Asia.

[14] 'Ramos signs military modernisation law', Agence France Presse, 23 Feb. 1995, cited in Snyder, C. A., Canadian Consortium on Asia Pacific Security (CANCAPS), *Making Mischief in the South China Sea*, CANCAPS Paper no. 7 (Center for International and Strategic Studies, York University: York, Ont., Aug. 1995), p. 14.

[15] Singh (note 4), p. 223.

Third, labelling regional arms procurement as simple 'modernization' seems to be a semantic distinction. While many capabilities are being modernized, it would seem to be more than a modernization when significant new capabilities are involved. This assessment is supported by the debate in the USA over South-East Asian acquisition of the AIM-120A AMRAAM (advanced medium-range air-to-air missile system), a beyond-visual-range weapon that significantly enhances capability:

[In justifying a sale to Thailand] US industry officials argue that missiles equivalent to the AMRAAM already are being flown by Thailand's neighbours. Malaysia, for example, has acquired Russian MiG-29 fighters equipped to launch the AA-12, often dubbed the AMRAAM-ski by US representatives. France's recent sale of the Mirage 2000-5 to Taiwan included 500 Mica missiles, which manufacturer Matra Defence-Espace, Velizy, touts as a lighter, cheaper version of AMRAAM.[16]

The arms acquisitions of course build on a fairly small base, and their extent is unlikely to cause concern for the extra-regional neighbours, such as China, the two Koreas or Taiwan. Clearly it is also in the interests of stability that South-East Asia should have adequate defence capabilities. However, the acquisition of modern, capable weapon systems should proceed in a way that does not cause concern for the region itself:

It is the internal balance matrix which will have the most serious implications for ASEAN. The ASEAN build-up can be potentially destabilizing because the four major powers in ASEAN—Singapore, Thailand, Malaysia and [Indonesia]—are evenly matched in terms of conventional military power. Intra-ASEAN stability can, furthermore, be undermined by historical animosities and suspicions. All the ASEAN states belong to the 'junior arms league', and are therefore all potential competitors. The fact that much of ASEAN defence planning is based on contingency planning can be detrimental to stability.
While the build-up has not become an arms race, it must be recognised that the greatest impact of the ASEAN arms program is internal. Consequently, it could be potentially destabilizing if the modernisation programs are not monitored or moderated.[17]

---

[16] Hitchens, T., 'Thais use AMRAAM as US fighter buy lever', *Defense News*, 4–10 Sep. 1995, p. 3.
[17] Mak, J. N., 'The ASEAN naval buildup: implications for the regional order', *Pacific Review*, vol. 8, no. 2 (1995), p. 321.

As suggested by another analyst, the arms modernization process in South-East Asia is 'sibling rivalry more than anything else in a region where we are friends and enemies at the same time'.[18]

Acquisitions themselves are not intrinsically destabilizing, particularly if they satisfy legitimate non-threatening needs. If it is true that weakened or poorly defended states leave the door open to aggression and instability, then regional stability requires countries' independent (and by extension, the region's collective) military strength.[19] On the other hand, as indicated by the appendix to this volume, a significant priority is placed in the region on the current and future acquisition of advanced fighter and strike aircraft, as well as other planned acquisitions such as submarines and modern surface combatants armed with long-range anti-ship missiles.[20] With these increased capabilities, regional actors will wish to ensure that these acquisitions and the security environment in which they are placed contribute to stabilizing, rather than destabilizing, conditions. Further development of confidence building in the region could strengthen this process.

IV. Building confidence and trust

Measures are needed to defuse the tensions and concerns surrounding ASEAN arms acquisitions. The former Malaysian Defence Minister, Najib Razak, delivering the keynote address at a maritime confidence-building measures (CBMs) seminar in Kuala Lumpur in August 1994, publicly welcomed the establishment of the ARF as 'beginning the process of institutionalising CBMs'.[21] That process has continued, and has led to the derivation of a comprehensive plan for the development of CBMs, preventive diplomacy and conflict-resolution mechanisms. The ARF itself significantly advances regional security by providing a regular forum for senior government representatives and senior officials to address security issues.

[18] Cited in Glashow, J. and Hitchens, T., 'Booming Pacific rim sparks arms export debate', *Defense News*, 4–10 Sep. 1995, p. 34.

[19] 'Legitimate' and 'unwarranted' arms acquisitions are further discussed in the South-East Asian context in chapter 6 in this volume.

[20] For a discussion of why these acquisitions are a cause for concern, see Ball, D., *Trends in Military Acquisitions in the Asia–Pacific Region: Implications for Security and Prospects for Constraints and Controls*, Working Paper no. 273 (Australian National University, Strategic and Defence Studies Centre: Canberra, 1993), pp. 20–21.

[21] Najib Razak, 'CBMs at sea in the Asia Pacific region: meeting the challenges of the 21st century', Keynote address at a MIMA seminar, Kuala Lumpur, 2 Aug. 1994.

The ARF Concept Paper, circulated in advance of the Second ARF meeting, held in Brunei in August 1995,[22] provided lists of measures recommended for adoption either 'in the immediate future' or for longer-term study in the areas of confidence building, preventive diplomacy, non-proliferation and arms control, peacekeeping and maritime security cooperation. These topic areas will now be considered in track-one and track-two forums, including ARF intersessional seminars, for further development and implementation.[23] On the question of arms transfer registers, the ARF has recommended regional accession to the UN Register of Conventional Arms and further study of a regional register. Some of the suggested measures are already in place or are covered by existing international protocols or procedures and some are of more diplomatic than operational utility. Nevertheless, they represent a substantial level of commitment to identifying practical CBMs, if not yet to implementing them.

The security environment in South-East Asia has both traditional and novel aspects. Because of the historical importance of trade, even in colonial times, and its geography, the region has always been a predominantly maritime region, but only since the entry into force of the UNCLOS has the requirement to extend economic jurisdiction out to 200 nautical miles been mandatory. Rivalries in the region have always been present. External powers are now preoccupied with establishing commercial success through investment and trade—including arms sales—rather than with imposing colonial rule. This external power interest has the potential to sharpen regional rivalries and add to the uncertainty of the regional security environment.

The product of these traditional and modern forces is to generate substantial capability enhancements within ASEAN. In many cases equipment acquisitions can be justified through consideration of the strategic circumstances peculiar to the country under consideration, but some acquisitions are less explicable. For these a transparency regime may be required which will defuse the tensions associated with enhanced capabilities.

---

[22] ASEAN, 'The ASEAN Regional Forum: A Concept Paper', attached to the Chairman's statement of the Second ASEAN Regional Forum (ARF), Aug. 1995, Bandar Seri Begawan (Brunei).

[23] See also chapter 5 in this volume.

4. The 'ASEAN way' and transparency in South-East Asia

J. N. Mak

I. Introduction

In ASEAN, while the notion of regional arms transparency mechanisms has gained support from a few members of the ruling élites, there has been no rigorous attempt to look at how such efforts will or can fit into the regional scheme of things.[1] Some basic questions will have to be asked. The two most fundamental of these are the focus of this chapter. The first is whether ASEAN needs a transparency mechanism such as a register of conventional arms. The second is whether the ASEAN tradition of cooperation and conflict management can form the basis of a process which might result in a regional arms trade transparency regime.

The ASEAN system is in many respects an exclusive one, and this is in itself a problem: it is transparent only to privileged members or insiders. The ASEAN system and its multilateral security experience are somewhat at variance with the notion of common security and transparency. This has implications for an arms register such as the United Nations Register of Conventional Arms (UNROCA), which belongs very much to the public domain.

Three major reasons account for the incompatibility of the 'ASEAN way' and complete transparency. First, the grouping in security terms is an inward-looking community. Conceptually, ASEAN security until the end of the cold war was based on what Michael Leifer described as 'collective internal security'.[2] Second, ASEAN has always been a very loosely structured organization marked by a lack of institutional procedures. It has always preferred bilateral linkages and solutions to

---

[1] A preliminary survey of the terrain has been undertaken by the International Working Group on Confidence and Security Building Measures of the Council for Security Cooperation in the Asia Pacific (CSCAP). Cossa, R. A. (ed.), *Toward a Regional Arms Register in the Asia Pacific* (Pacific Forum CSIS: Honolulu, Aug. 1995). See also Mak, J. N., *ASEAN Defence Re-orientation 1975–1992: The Dynamics of Modernisation and Structural Change*, Canberra Papers on Strategy and Defence (Australian National University, Strategic and Defence Studies Centre: Canberra, 1994).

[2] Leifer, M., *ASEAN and the Security of South-East Asia* (Routledge: London, 1989), pp. 66–67.

problems. This is at variance with the multilateral structured approach which characterizes the UNROCA. Finally, ASEAN has never had a tradition of multilateral openness, preferring to negotiate and resolve conflicts quietly, away from the public eye.

Section II of this chapter examines the demands that transparency would make on ASEAN and analyses whether the ASEAN way can be reconciled with those demands. Section III considers different types of arms register in the regional context and section IV argues the case for promoting the debate on the suitability of transparency as a confidence-building measure (CBM) in South-East Asia.

II. Arms, multilateralism and the ASEAN way

Arms acquisitions and stability

The ASEAN countries have gone through three phases of arms acquisitions. The first was in the 1960s, followed by a second phase from approximately the end of the 1970s to the mid-1980s. The third and latest phase started around 1987. This third phase, characterized by its maritime focus and greatly enhanced capability, is well documented.[3]

This round of arms acquisitions has been variously described as defence modernization, as building up a minimal defence capability and as an arms race. The region's defence acquisitions in the 1990s have the most potential to upset the intra-ASEAN balance of power, while their impact on the wider Asia–Pacific region will probably be minimal. This is because the number of new weapons being acquired is insignificant compared to the order of battle of countries such as China, Japan, the two Koreas and Taiwan. Within ASEAN itself, however, the new systems acquired or on order represent significant increases in terms of quantity as well as quality. Thus this could have serious implications for ASEAN and South-East Asian stability.[4] Nevertheless some writers take regional stability in South-East Asia for granted and are quite dismissive of the idea of a regional arms register.[5]

---

[3] Ball, D., 'Arms and affluence: military acquisitions in the Asia–Pacific region', *International Security*, vol. 18, no. 3 (winter 1993/94).

[4] Mak, J. N., 'The ASEAN naval build-up: implications for the regional order', *Pacific Review*, vol. 8, no. 2 (1995).

[5] One regional analyst noted that an arms register 'would not be a particularly urgent or even important confidence-building or arms control measure' because South-East Asia is not

Given that intra-ASEAN tensions and suspicions still exist, a strong case can be made for the introduction of CBMs to complement the traditional conflict-management approach of ASEAN.[6] Moreover, ASEAN multilateralism in the post-cold war era is not about managing the wider regional order, but about sustaining cohesiveness in an enlarged and possibly different ASEAN. One measure which could contribute to intra-ASEAN confidence building is a regional arms trade transparency mechanism such as a register. A register would, at the very minimum, make all ASEAN arms acquisitions known to all its members at the official level, if not publicly. This would help to ensure that any build-up would be monitored and, it can be hoped, prevented from becoming destabilizing; but can such an approach be implemented within the ASEAN way?

Much of the present stability in ASEAN is based on bilateral links based on close personal ties. Given that regional leaders will not live forever, there is a need for institutional structures that will survive their passing. A mechanism is also needed to deal with the political disputes which can develop virtually overnight among regional states.

The ASEAN approach to multilateralism

Arms transparency regimes are part of common security as defined by the Palme Commission.[7] In recent years ASEAN has moved away from its espousal of strictly bilateral, intra-ASEAN security ties to what appear to be more multilateral and slightly more structured security relationships. This is reflected in the establishment of the ARF, which represents ASEAN's first formal multilateral security effort but is in its earliest stages of development.

particularly nervous about arms acquisitions and defence expenditure. Mohamed Jawhar B. Hassan, 'An Asia Pacific arms register: utility and prospects', ed. Cossa (note 1), p. 43.

[6] Acharya, A., International Institute for Strategic Studies, *A New Regional Order in South-East Asia: ASEAN in the Post-Cold War Era*, Adelphi Paper no. 279 (Brassey's: Oxford, 1993), pp. 75–76; and Muthiah, A., 'Regionalism and the quest for security: ASEAN and the Cambodian conflict', *Australian Journal of International Affairs*, vol. 47, no. 2 (Oct. 1993), p. 211.

[7] Independent Commission on Disarmament and Security Issues, *Common Security: A Programme for Disarmament* (Pan Books: London, 1982). 'Cooperative security' as defined by David B. Dewitt is often used as synonymous. This is a Canadian concept which is all-inclusive. It is characterized by a process 'to establish habits of dialogue' supported by track-two diplomacy. Dewitt, D. B., 'Concepts of security for the Asia–Pacific region in the post-cold war era', Paper presented at the Seventh Asia Pacific Roundtable, Kuala Lumpur, 6–9 June 1993.

Important elements of preventive diplomacy appear to be part of the ASEAN tradition. Indeed, one of the primary avowed purposes of ASEAN, embodied in the Bangkok Declaration of 1967, is the 'promotion of regional peace and stability'.[8] The 1976 ASEAN Treaty of Amity and Cooperation also eschews the use of force in resolving disputes and emphasizes non-interference in the internal affairs of members. While security and stability have been major aims of ASEAN, the internal and domestic affairs of each country are deemed to be sacrosanct and inviolable. This latter belief could have important implications for transparency.

In this respect, the security concept expounded by ASEAN has been essentially focused on collective internal security. This notion internalizes security to a high degree. The 1976 Declaration of ASEAN Concord maintained that 'the stability of each member state and of the ASEAN region is an essential contribution to international peace and security. Each member state resolves to eliminate threats posed by subversion to its stability, thus strengthening national and ASEAN resilience'.[9] The concept of comprehensive security found great favour among individual ASEAN states for its emphasis on internal or national resilience. Comprehensive security takes a total approach to national security: threats are not only military but include political, economic and socio-cultural threats at various levels and both domestic and international threats.[10] Comprehensive security was the path to collective internal security—more commonly referred to in ASEAN circles as 'national/regional resilience'. This concept derives directly from the Indonesian concept of *ketahanan nasional* and is more inward-looking than other notions of comprehensive security.[11]

Because of this internalized ASEAN approach the notion of transparency and open reassurance demanded by common security could be a difficulty. A degree of dissonance emerges even at the conceptual level between traditional ASEAN security concepts and the transparency demands of common security.

[8] ASEAN, The ASEAN Declaration, Bangkok, 8 Aug. 1967.
[9] Cited in Leifer (note 2), p. 66.
[10] Muthiah, A., 'Comprehensive security: interpretations in ASEAN countries', eds R. A. Scalapino *et al.*, *Asian Security Issues: Regional and Global* (Institute of East Asian Studies, University of California: Berkeley, Calif., 1988), p. 57. Some analysts have equated the ASEAN concept of national resilience with comprehensive security. However, there is a distinction. National resilience is a concept for regime stability, since it includes political stability and a sense of nationalism among its goals. Irvine, D., 'Making haste slowly: ASEAN from 1975', ed. A. Broinowski, *Understanding ASEAN* (Macmillan: London, 1982).

The ASEAN way

Much has been written about the ASEAN way of conflict resolution and conflict management.[12] In essence it is a dialogue characterized by the following key features:

1. It is unstructured. ASEAN itself was inaugurated without any clearly defined or formal structure. The process of negotiation is therefore informal, with no clear format for decision making, much less for implementing policies.

2. There is little formal agenda apart from scheduled meetings. Instead, negotiations tend to circle around specific issues as they arise.

3. It is essentially a consensus-building and negotiating process characterized by two features: *musyawarah* and *mufakat. Musyawarah* is the process of decision making through consultation and discussion; *mufakat* refers to the unanimous decision reached.[13]

4. Unanimity is deemed central to ASEAN conflict management. This characteristic of consensus building results in policies which reflect an amalgamation of the most acceptable views of each and every member. In ASEAN negotiations all parties have power over each other.

5. Decision making is usually a protracted matter, simply because of the need to arrive at mutually acceptable decisions.[14] Issues are therefore discussed with no fixed timetable or agenda. The only condition is that the issues must be resolved to the satisfaction of all the parties involved, however long that might take.

6. The ASEAN process is largely an exclusive, closed one. Negotiations are essentially behind the scenes, if not secretive, involving only key officials working on specific issues. The ASEAN way therefore lacks transparency at the public level. Historically it distinguishes between outsiders and insiders: ASEAN decided early on that closed-door negotiations would be the order of the day because 'national rep-

---

[11] Dewitt (note 7), p. 8.

[12] For comprehensive descriptions of the ASEAN way, see Kamarulzaman, A., 'ASEAN and conflict management: the formative years of 1967–1976', *Pacific Review*, vol. 6, no. 2 (1994); and Thambipillai, P. and Saravanamuttu, J., *ASEAN Negotiations: Two Insights* (Institute of Southeast Asian Studies: Singapore, 1985).

[13] Thambipillai and Saravanamuttu (note 12), p. 11.

[14] Thambipillai and Saravanamuttu (note 12), p. 6.

resentatives can negotiate and consult each other freely without being obliged to defend their position in public'.[15]

7. A tacit agreement prevails to avoid sensitive issues. This sometimes results in problems being hidden rather than resolved. For example, outstanding intra-ASEAN tensions such as those between Malaysia and Singapore are seldom aired officially.

8. Most ASEAN interaction takes place at the bilateral level, a point particularly true of security linkages. There is virtually no multilateral defence or security forum. Exceptions include a multilateral annual seminar on intelligence exchange. In nearly all other areas, such as military exercises, ASEAN has firmly kept to the bilateral format.

Transparency versus the ASEAN way

This discussion indicates that a number of incompatibilities stand between the ASEAN approach to multilateral security and the public transparency required for the establishment of an effective transparency mechanism for arms trade and defence-related issues. First, at a fundamental level, ASEAN states would have to agree that transparency would benefit all participants and make a positive contribution to confidence building. Even if agreement could be reached at that stage, further agreement would be needed on certain specifics, such as the form and nature of the transparency mechanism. In addition, consensus would be needed as to early-warning indicators and how they would be discussed in order to monitor and avoid potentially destabilizing build-ups. This process of consensus building and agreement would be a long one and could be derailed by any ASEAN member if and when it so wished.

Second, the notion of public transparency seems to be at variance with the ASEAN tradition of quiet, almost secretive, behind-the-scenes diplomacy. Not only are the multilateral discussions secretive, but so are policies and decisions at the national level within most ASEAN states. In terms of openness the ASEAN countries range from the liberal Philippines, where little is secret, to highly sensitive Singapore, where virtually anything military would be secret. To complicate matters, the entry of Viet Nam into ASEAN means that the ASEAN process of achieving consensus now involves a traditionally

---

[15] Kamarulzaman (note 12), p. 64.

closed and secretive communist government. The entry of Cambodia, Laos and Myanmar would complicate matters even more.

Third, even the broad notion of common security is something relatively new for ASEAN. Although the concept has arguably gained limited acceptance, many regional élites (including key ASEAN officials) are still more at home with the ASEAN tradition of running a closed, exclusive group where openness is confined to the members of the 'club'. Just as Western societies have their cold warriors struggling to come to terms with the post-cold war world, so too many members of the ASEAN élites face the psychological transition from interacting within an exclusive ASEAN club where links have been established largely on a bilateral basis and chosen without compulsion to interacting in common to the challenges of a more multipolar and demanding world.[16]

III. Approaches to arms-related transparency

Is the concept of a meaningful ASEAN arms-related transparency mechanism therefore doomed at the outset? Not necessarily.

Given the difficulties and sensitivities described above, four possible approaches might be presented for the development of greater arms-related transparency at the ASEAN, or regional, level.

A closed ASEAN arms register

A closed arms register would only be transparent to the ASEAN members themselves and would not be incompatible with the ASEAN way. Indeed, it would be part of the ASEAN tradition. Because of this it would perhaps be the most acceptable official register. However, there are drawbacks to such a solution. In the first place, it would not be fully consistent with the concept of public transparency. Because it would be closed it would have limited utility as a model for the rest of the world. It would also be seen as being out of step with the wider regional move towards cooperative security.

More importantly, a closed arms register would constrain academics, analysts and the rest of the world community working on disarmament and arms control issues from providing inputs and constructive criticism. ASEAN alone may not have the expertise to

---

[16] Acharya (note 6), p. 74.

develop the parameters and indicators for determining stabilizing/destabilizing thresholds in arms acquisitions. Nevertheless, a closed register would still be a good start.

A 'non-ASEAN' ASEAN arms register

One way out of the consensus dilemma would be to adopt the ASEAN way itself. Whenever ASEAN reached an impasse on particular issues which did not necessarily jeopardize the cohesiveness of the grouping it would take action outside the purview of ASEAN. In this sense it would be possible to jump-start the transparency process by persuading like-minded members of ASEAN to take part in a South-East Asian transparency regime. Such an arrangement would involve ASEAN states but would not involve ASEAN directly.

The Philippines would be one obvious candidate to participate in such a process, while Malaysia and Thailand might have no serious reservations about the concept of regional arms-related transparency measures. This approach seems limited, but it is limited only in terms of numbers. The core group of members could still go through the entire intellectual and methodological exercise of developing a sub-regional arms register and give an example for non-participating ASEAN member states and the rest of the region of what a conventional arms register can or cannot achieve. Depending on the outcome of such a limited experiment, the rest of the region might decide for or against participation.

The problem with this approach is that states with the most to hide, and which have the most problems with transparency, would probably refuse to participate. In this sense such a limited register could eventually be a self-defeating exercise.

A de facto regional arms register

The idea of a non-official de facto arms register should not be dismissed. Even if an official regional arms register is implemented, a non-official track-two exercise would still be valuable in verifying 'hits and misses' in reporting and in refining methodological approaches, including which categories of weapons would have the greatest regional impact on stability.[17]

In the case of ASEAN, a de facto register such as the MIMA–SIPRI report[18] or the register provided in the appendix to this volume could form the basis for a semi-official arms register. By encouraging the cooperation of officials and scholars working outside the official realm, the basic foundation of a de facto register could be refined to the point of being as accurate as an official register. This might eventually persuade ruling élites to participate officially in this process of common security. Indeed, it may be suspected that it will be at the academic level that most progress in methodological approaches in developing arms registers will be achieved. Maintaining a de facto arms register thus makes good intellectual sense, besides contributing to the common security process.

A register for specific arms categories

Another approach would be to establish a transparency regime to capture information on armaments considered most destabilizing to the region. For example, in the case of ASEAN and the Asia–Pacific region this might involve a special focus on offensive maritime capabilities. The advantage of such an approach is that countries would not be required to reveal everything in their defence inventories. The challenge is to define categories of weapons considered to have the greatest impact on regional stability.

Since maritime arms, particularly warships, are by nature not easy to hide, there is already an element of in-built transparency. However, the problem would be to persuade participating states to report the types of sub-systems such as anti-ship missiles embarked on maritime platforms. Systems can make a difference in determining the defensive or offensive capabilities of a certain platform. There are thus serious problems to overcome to make a limited register effective. On balance, however, the idea of such a register is attractive since it could

[17] Such an effort has been undertaken in 2 studies which compare open-source data with the official returns of the UN Register. Laurance, E. J., Wezeman, S. T. and Wulf, H., *Arms Watch: SIPRI Report on the First Year of the UN Register of Conventional Arms*, SIPRI Research Report no. 6 (Oxford University Press: Oxford 1993); and Sislin, J. and Wezeman, S. T., *1994 Arms Transfers: A Register of Deliveries from Public Sources* (Monterey Institute of International Studies: Monterey, Calif., Mar. 1995).

[18] Gill, B., Mak, J. N. and Wezeman, S., *ASEAN Arms Acquisitions: Developing Transparency* (MIMA: Kuala Lumpur, Aug. 1995).

include states which are prepared to cooperate only in very limited ways with the hope of further expanding its scope at a future date.

IV. Conclusions

It would be tempting to say that the concept of a meaningful register of conventional arms is incompatible with the ASEAN multilateral culture and tradition. It would also be easy to argue that the notion of an arms register would be difficult to develop in the region. More than that, there is the temptation to take the easy way out by assuming that there are no intra-ASEAN security tensions which cannot be resolved by the traditional ASEAN way of conflict management and negotiations and that an ASEAN arms register is therefore irrelevant and unnecessary.

As noted above, reliance on the traditional ASEAN conflict-management approach has several disadvantages. There is good reason, therefore, to complement the ASEAN way with confidence-building and early-warning mechanisms which can be effective irrespective of who is in charge or how good relations between counterparts in the ASEAN official community may be. If ASEAN wishes to play a leading role in the ARF and to be on the cutting edge of cooperative security, then it must be prepared to deal with extremely difficult and challenging concepts.[19]

One way to address these challenges is to generate a debate among regional experts and officials on whether arms-related transparency is needed in the region and, if it is, in what form it is needed. If the conclusion is that transparency could undermine regional security then either the level of intra-ASEAN tensions must be higher than initially envisaged or there could be latent distrust between the ASEAN grouping and other regional states such as China. Other confidence-building measures apart from transparency should then be examined for their potential contribution to regional stability. On the other hand, if arms transparency measures are deemed to be potentially stabilizing

---

[19] One of the region's most distinguished security analysts argues that a goal for ARF should be to create an *active regional institution in arms control and disarmament and non-proliferation activities* (emphasis added). Wanandi, J., 'The future of ARF and CSCAP in the regional security architecture', Paper presented at the Eighth Asia Pacific Roundtable, Kuala Lumpur, June 1994, pp. 8–10. More recently he has argued that non-proliferation and arms control should be among the 3 main tasks of the ARF. Wanandi, J., 'The ARF: objectives, process and programmes', Paper presented at the Ninth Asia Pacific Roundtable, Kuala Lumpur, 5–8 June 1995, p. 5.

then the challenge would be to move ahead and refine the concept so that the regional register can provide the indicators needed to assess when a build-up is excessive and destabilizing. Careful analysis and debate are needed to determine what form transparency might take, with the several approaches raised above, among others, being taken into consideration.[20]

Given the changing nature of the security environment in South-East Asia, regional security will be best served if this type of debate and discussion starts sooner rather than later. The preliminary ideas suggested here and throughout this volume are first steps in this debate and can contribute to and support discussions on arms, transparency and security at the official level in ASEAN, South-East Asia and the wider Asia–Pacific region.[21]

[20] Regardless of the outcome of the transparency debate in ASEAN and the ARF, a de facto register should be maintained within track two. A de facto register—such as Gill, Mak and Wezeman (note 18)—could advance the conceptual debate on the link between transparency and security within the wider context of cooperative security and could support specific studies at both the academic and the official levels.

[21] The ARF has expressed its support for regional defence-related transparency and the unofficial track-two process has actively considered such transparency in the Asia–Pacific region. However, as argued in chapter 1, ASEAN will need to take the lead for such measures to take effective shape in the wider region.

5. Defence cooperation and transparency in South-East Asia

Amitav Acharya

I. Introduction

The countries of South-East Asia and particularly those in ASEAN have focused on military modernization while at the same time leading the development of a new regional security framework for the Asia–Pacific region. ASEAN governments insist that their military build-up is a modest modernization effort but have also stressed the need for preventive measures, such as regional arms- and defence-related transparency measures, to ensure greater mutual trust and confidence. How feasible are transparency measures in South-East Asia?

ASEAN has already developed an approach to regional security which often differs from Western approaches and has proved relatively effective as a confidence-building tool in South-East Asia. This chapter looks at that track record of intra-ASEAN security and defence cooperation in order to ascertain whether some of the factors that have shaped ASEAN's attitude towards intramural defence ties can also be relevant to its likely response to the current need for military transparency and to the feasibility of enhanced regional transparency measures. Section II traces the evolution of defence cooperation within ASEAN and examines the various forms of bilateral ties that have developed among its members. Section III examines the objectives and functions of defence bilateralism and its contribution to regional security and section IV assesses the relevance of the ASEAN experience to developing defence information-sharing and transparency measures for the region.

II. The evolution of defence cooperation in ASEAN

Since its creation in 1967, ASEAN has developed a range of defence ties. These include border region cooperation, intelligence sharing, joint exercises, exchanges at military education and training institutes, frequent senior-level official visits, provision of combat training facilities and limited cooperation in the defence industrial sector. However, these forms of defence cooperation have overwhelmingly been undertaken on a bilateral basis. The rationale for defence bilateralism was clearly restated by a former Chief of the Malaysian Armed Forces, General Hashim Mohammed Ali:

Bilateral defence cooperation is flexible and provide[s] wide ranging options. It allows any ASEAN partner to decide the type, time and scale of aid it requires and can provide. The question of national independence and sovereignty is unaffected by the decision of others as in the case of an alliance where members can [invoke] the terms of the treaty and interfere in the affairs of another partner.[1]

The emergence of bilateral defence cooperation among the ASEAN countries predates the birth of ASEAN in 1967 and can be divided into three main periods.

Phase I: the formative years

The initial stimulus for defence cooperation within ASEAN came from the threat of communist insurgency. Such cooperation included the formation of joint border committees, combined operations to control the trans-boundary movement of subversive elements and the sharing of intelligence information about insurgencies. The oldest bilateral border security arrangement, between Malaysia and Thailand, dates back to 1949.[2] Indonesia and the Philippines signed a Border Crossing Agreement in May 1961 followed by a Joint Border Patrol Agreement in 1975.[3] The 1975 agreement covered smuggling, illegal fishing and immigration, piracy and drug trafficking and the two sides organized coordinated naval patrols in the waterway between southern Mindanao and northern Sulawesi involving patrol

---

[1] Ali, H. A. (Gen.), 'Regional defence from the military perspective', *ISIS Focus*, no. 58 (Jan. 1990), pp. 41–42.

[2] These agreements are: Thai–Malayan Police Frontier Agreement (1949); Agreement on Border Operations against Communist Terrorists between the Government of Thailand and the Government of the Federation of Malaya (1959); Agreement between the Government of Thailand and the Government of Malaysia on Border Cooperation (1965); Agreement between the Government of Thailand and the Government of Malaysia on Border Cooperation (1970); and Agreement between the Government of Malaysia and the Government of Thailand on Border Cooperation (1977). Kuntom, R., 'Bilateral border security cooperation between Malaysia and Thailand', Paper presented to the First Annual Thailand–Malaysia Colloquium, Bangkok, 2–3 Sep. 1987, pp. 2–3.

[3] *Straits Times*, 26 May 1977.

craft and maritime reconnaissance aircraft.[4] The basic framework for Indonesia–Malaysia border cooperation was the Bangkok Agreement of May 1966 in which joint operations against border-region communists were 'agreed upon without any formal agreement being signed'.[5] This understanding was followed by an exchange of letters in March 1967. In 1972 the two countries signed a Border Security Agreement which was revised and expanded in 1984.[6] While Malaysia and the Philippines signed a border agreement in 1977,[7] little progress was made because of their dispute over Sabah.

Along with border cooperation agreements, a number of bilateral intelligence-sharing arrangements emerged between the ASEAN members during the late 1960s and 1970s as a result of the worsening situation in Indo-China and the rising threat of communist subversion. A significant aspect of these arrangements was the fact that some involved countries which were not part of formal bilateral border security agreements such as those between Malaysia and Thailand or Malaysia and Indonesia. Intelligence sharing, which later included an ASEAN-wide multilateral meeting of the member states' intelligence organizations, thus provided an alternative form of security collaboration against the threat of insurgency and subversion within ASEAN.

The new US regional security posture articulated in 1969, the Nixon Doctrine, impressed on the ASEAN states the need for greater self-reliance, prompting some debate as to whether collective security was desirable or feasible. Furthermore, the US withdrawal from Viet Nam in 1973 and the subsequent communist victories in Indo-China led to renewed calls for greater military cooperation within ASEAN. At its first summit meeting, however, held in Bali in 1976, ASEAN reaffirmed the position that security cooperation would remain outside the ASEAN framework. The Declaration of ASEAN Concord issued at Bali gave formal expression to this position by calling for 'continuation of cooperation on a non-ASEAN basis between member states in security matters in accordance with their mutual needs and interests'. Summing up the position reached at Bali regarding security cooperation, the Malaysian Prime Minister, Hussein Onn, stated:

[4] Personal interview with the Philippine Defence Attaché, Jakarta, 10 Aug. 1989.

[5] Rahman, T. A., 'Indonesian peace mission', *The Star* (Petaling Jaya), 15 Aug. 1983.

[6] 'Malaysia/Indonesia security arrangements', *Foreign Affairs Malaysia*, vol. 5, no. 2 (June 1972); Djiwandono, S., 'Regional security cooperation: an ASEAN perspective', *Pacific Regional Security: The 1985 Pacific Symposium* (National Defense University Press: Washington, DC, 1988), p. 534; and *New Straits Times*, 29 Nov. 1985.

[7] *Asian Security, 1981* (Research Institute for Peace and Security: Tokyo, 1980), p. 120.

It is obvious that ASEAN member states do not wish to change the character of ASEAN as a socio-economic organisation into a security alliance as this would only create misunderstanding in the region and undermine the positive achievements of ASEAN in promoting peace and stability through socio-economic and related fields . . . [The Bali summit meeting] reiterated the nature of ASEAN as a non-ideological, non-military and non-antagonistic grouping.[8]

Phase II: the Cambodia conflict, 1979–89

While defence cooperation in the first phase revolved primarily around border cooperation and intelligence sharing, cooperation in the second phase featured joint exercises, training and, to a lesser extent, defence industrial cooperation. ASEAN's rejection of defence multi-lateralism was seriously tested by the Vietnamese invasion of Cambodia in 1978, which made Thailand ASEAN's front-line state. Some senior ASEAN statesmen, such as Adam Malik, a former foreign minister of Indonesia who had earlier opposed a military role for ASEAN, now proposed that ASEAN should demonstrate its unity by holding joint military exercises on the Thai–Cambodian border.[9] While pledges were made by Indonesia, Malaysia and Singapore to provide contingency support to Thailand, a framework for ASEAN-wide security cooperation against external threats proved to be elusive. Any temptation to form a joint military arrangement to provide contingency support to Thailand against Viet Nam was tempered by the fact that ASEAN lacked the collective ability to stand up to an all-out Vietnamese attack. As Lee Kuan Yew, former prime minister of Singapore, warned: 'there is no combination of forces in South-East Asia that can stop the Vietnamese on the mainland of Asia'.[10]

More importantly, the differing perspectives within ASEAN on the Sino-Vietnamese rivalry, telescoped by the Cambodia crisis, proved to be a major barrier to greater intra-ASEAN political and security cooperation. Unlike Singapore and Thailand, Indonesia and Malaysia held the view that it was China, rather than the Soviet Union or Viet Nam, which posed the most serious long-term threat to regional security and stability. Their recognition of Viet Nam's potential as a

---

[8] *New Straits Times*, 11 Jan. 1978.

[9] *The Star* (Petaling Jaya), 9 May 1984.

[10] Cited in Garcia, R. C., 'Military cooperation in ASEAN', *The Pointer* (Singapore), Apr.–June 1987, p. 9.

'countervailing force against China'[11] meant eschewing a military role for ASEAN which would have provoked and further alienated Viet Nam at a time when both Indonesia and Malaysia continued to harbour hopes of an eventual *rapprochement* with Hanoi.

Another factor which influenced ASEAN's thinking on defence cooperation was the development of an alliance relationship between the Soviet Union and Viet Nam in the 1980s. This was alarming to ASEAN leaders who regarded it as a threat to the balance of power in the region. Lee Kuan Yew provided the clearest expression of this concern. At a press conference in Jakarta on 9 November 1982, he advocated an expansion of existing bilateral military exercises to 'multilateral exercises encompassing all the [ASEAN] members'.[12] Lee's suggestion was rejected by fellow ASEAN members, with Indonesia reiterating its view that existing bilateral linkages between ASEAN states were sufficient to deal with emerging security threats and that any multilateral exercises would be 'similar to ASEAN opening a new front', and would provoke the 'other side'.[13]

Despite the rejection of multilateral defence cooperation, bilateral defence ties within ASEAN intensified in the 1980s. Border exercises with a counter-insurgency focus were joined by air and naval exercises with a conventional warfare orientation. Examples of such exercises include the Malapura naval exercises between Singapore and Malaysia and the Indopura naval exercises between Singapore and Indonesia. Bilateral army exercises, initially resisted because they might allow the security forces of the guest country to familiarize themselves with the territory of the host nation, were instituted much later in the late 1980s with the Safkar Indopura exercises between Indonesia and Singapore and the Semangat Bersatu series between Malaysia and Singapore. ASEAN countries were also involved in cooperation in the area of training and exchange of facilities. Singapore was the main beneficiary of such cooperation, maintaining army training camps in Thailand[14] and Brunei[15] and a detachment of fighter

---

[11] Hernandez, C., 'Regional security in ASEAN: a Philippine perspective', Paper presented to the Asiatic Research Centre Conference on East Asian Security: Perceptions and Realities, Korea University, Seoul, 25–26 May 1984, p. 12.

[12] Cited in Richardson, M., 'ASEAN extends its military ties', *Pacific Defence Reporter*, Nov. 1982, p. 55.

[13] *New Straits Times*, 17 Sep. 1982.

[14] *Bangkok Post*, 17 July 1983; and *New Straits Times*, 18 July 1983.

[15] *Straits Times*, 22 Aug. 1986.

aircraft at the Clark Air Force Base in the Philippines.[16] The Royal Thai Air Force used the Crow Valley range in the Philippines for air weapon testing purposes,[17] while Bangkok offered military training facilities to Brunei.[18] In addition ASEAN members allowed and encouraged participation of students from other ASEAN countries in the military education and officer training programmes at their national military institutions. The most important form of such interaction involved the service command and staff colleges used to train middle- and senior-level officers. Apart from exchanges at the command and staff level, ASEAN armed forces developed ties in the area of tactical training. Thailand and Singapore exchanged troops for commando training, while Malaysian troops trained at the Indonesian special forces training school at Batu Djajar and Malaysia's Jungle and Combat Warfare School in Johore accepted trainees from other ASEAN states, including officers from Singapore.[19]

Another area of intra-ASEAN defence ties which was broached during this period related to defence industrial cooperation and joint procurement of weapons. Indonesia had been an early advocate of ASEAN cooperation in defence industrialization, which it viewed as an essential response to the strategic situation arising from the US withdrawal from Indo-China. In 1978 General Maradan Panggabean, Indonesia's Coordinating Minister for Security and General Policies, suggested the establishment of an ASEAN arms factory.[20] In the aftermath of the Vietnamese invasion of Cambodia, Thailand explored but ultimately rejected the possibility of an ASEAN 'war reserve contingency pool'.[21] In 1984 Indonesia and Malaysia reportedly agreed to set up a joint consultative committee to look into the possibility of purchasing aircraft, spare parts and other military items,[22] although the proposal went no further than this.

Some standardization of weapon systems occurred among the ASEAN countries in the late 1970s and early 1980s, although this was

[16] Warner, D., 'Point, counterpoint in South China Sea', *Pacific Defence Reporter*, Aug. 1984, p. 54.

[17] Warner (note 16).

[18] *The Star* (Petaling Jaya), 30 Aug. 1984.

[19] Mak, J. N., *Directions for Greater Defence Cooperation* (Institute of Strategic and International Studies: Kuala Lumpur, 1986), p. 13.

[20] *New Straits Times*, 6 July 1978.

[21] Personal interview, Bangkok, 26 June 1989.

[22] *The Star* (Petaling Jaya), 17 July 1984.

not a conscious, coordinated effort. All except Brunei and Viet Nam acquired F-5 fighters and C-130 transport aircraft, while three (Indonesia, Malaysia and Singapore) acquired A-4 attack aircraft. The F-16 later entered service in the air forces of Indonesia, Singapore and Thailand. These three countries and Malaysia also introduced different versions of the Sidewinder air-to-air missile (AAM), while the Rapier surface-to-air missile (SAM) entered the inventories of Brunei, Indonesia and Singapore. In terms of naval weapons, the Exocet anti-ship missile was purchased by Indonesia, Malaysia and Thailand and later by Singapore. Commonality was also evident in ground forces equipment, Commando V-150 armoured personnel carriers (APCs) being acquired by Indonesia, Malaysia, the Philippines, Singapore and Thailand, while Brunei, Malaysia, the Philippines and Thailand introduced Scorpion light tanks to their inventories.

This apparent standardization was, however, not due to any conscious policy or design.[23] Opportunities for joint procurement from external suppliers, which might have resulted in significant cost savings, were ignored. For example, a joint procurement drive might have obtained better terms in the purchase of a multi-role fighter aircraft by Indonesia, Malaysia, Singapore and Thailand. As it was, Indonesia, Singapore and Thailand acquired the F-16A/B from the USA separately and Malaysia purchased the MiG-29 from the USSR and the F/A-18 from the USA.[24] ASEAN officials themselves were sceptical about the prospects for joint procurement, production and standardization.

Some of the most important barriers to greater ASEAN cooperation on joint weapon procurement are differences in military spending levels, geographic conditions, doctrine and overall military strategy, all of which lead to divergent procurement needs. Moreover, since ASEAN producers were not self-reliant in defence-related technologies, their interest in entering into joint ventures with external producers far exceeded their interest in creating an ASEAN industry. Lingering political suspicions among ASEAN states also affected the prospects for greater cooperation in defence production.[25] For

---

[23] Mak (note 19), p. 17.
[24] Karniol, R., 'ASEAN's need for greater defence cooperation', *Jane's Defence Weekly*, 10 Dec. 1988, p. 1495.
[25] Ahmed, Z. A., 'Asean countries should jointly produce weapons', *Far Eastern Economic Review*, 20 Feb. 1986, pp. 26–27.

example, the fear that an ASEAN arms manufacturing scheme might result in a leading role for Singapore, which would give the island republic undue leverage over its neighbours, may have been a constraining factor on intra-ASEAN cooperation in defence production.[26] These problems continue to weigh against the development of intra-ASEAN arms production or arms procurement schemes.

Phase III: post-cold war trends

Even with the end of the cold war, ASEAN has yet to embrace defence multilateralism while bilateral defence ties within ASEAN have developed even further. The opening of a 10 850-hectare joint air weapons testing range in Sumatra in March 1989, developed by Indonesia and Singapore, was an important example of such bilateralism.[27] Other ASEAN countries have also developed military ties through provision of training facilities. Malaysia and Singapore launched a bilateral security dialogue, called the Malaysia–Singapore Defence Forum, and signed a Memorandum of Understanding on defence industrial cooperation to involve co-production as well as joint marketing of defence equipment.[28] Bilateral defence industry cooperation was also evident in an agreement between Indonesia's PT Pindad and Singapore's Chartered Firearms Industries allowing the former to licence-produce Singapore's 40-mm automatic grenade launcher.[29] Malaysia and the Philippines overcame their long-standing dispute over Sabah to sign an agreement covering exchange of defence-related information, logistic support and training.[30] Singapore and the Philippines launched their first ever army exercises, code-

---

[26] In this context the conclusions of a US Central Intelligence Agency (CIA) study leaked to columnist Jack Anderson are interesting. The study contended that Singapore's defence industry 'if developed far enough could give Singapore leverage with neighbouring states by making them dependent on Singapore for needed spare parts and ammunition'. For a reference to this study, see Ho Kwon Ping and Cheah Cheng Hye, 'Five fingers on the trigger', *Far Eastern Economic Review*, 24 Oct. 1980, p. 37.

[27] 'Promoting bilateral cooperation between Singapore and Indonesia', *The Pioneer*, no. 138 (Apr. 1989), pp. 2–3; and *Straits Times*, 24 Mar. 1989.

[28] Karniol, R., 'Forum offers new era to Singapore/Malaysia', *Jane's Defence Weekly*, 28 Jan. 1995, p. 16; and 'The first Malaysia–Singapore Defence Forum', *Asian Defence Journal*, Mar. 1995, pp. 15–17.

[29] 'CIS 40-AGL to be built in Indonesia', *Jane's Defence Weekly*, 28 May 1994, p. 23.

[30] 'Defence co-operation', *Jane's Defence Weekly*, 8 Oct. 1994, p. 2.

named Anoa-Singa, in 1993.[31] Malaysia signed a Memorandum of Understanding with Indonesia to import six Indonesian-built CN-235 transport aircraft in return for Indonesia's purchase of 20 Malaysian-built SME MD3-160 trainer aircraft.[32]

Steps towards defence multilateralism have been extremely modest. On the one hand, Indonesia and Singapore have offered fellow ASEAN members access to their jointly developed Air Combat Manoeuvring Range (ACMR) near Pekan Baru in central Sumatra.[33] Furthermore, ASEAN has established a Special Working Group to discuss defence cooperation, the first formal grouping of defence officials from ASEAN member states. On the other hand, old barriers to defence multilateralism persist. A 1990 initiative to create a regional association of national defence industries of ASEAN states failed because of political and financial problems.[34] More recently, a Thai invitation to its ASEAN neighbours, as well as Australia, New Zealand and the USA, to participate in a new multilateral exercise fell through, although Singapore became the first outside country allowed to fully observe the US–Thai Cobra Gold military exercise.[35] Similarly, Malaysia's suggestion to establish an ASEAN peacekeeping force, based on the Nordic battalion model,[36] has received only limited support within ASEAN.[37]

A major new development in regional defence cooperation in South-East Asia is the emergence of bilateral ties between the non-communist ASEAN states and the Indo-Chinese countries, especially Viet Nam. Viet Nam's Deputy Foreign Minister indicated Hanoi's desire to promote cooperation with ASEAN partners 'in the field of national security and defence in mutually acceptable ways' with a

---

[31] 'Singapore–Philippines first bilateral army exercise', *Asian Defence Journal*, July 1994, p. 85.

[32] 'Paving the way to purchase of Indonesian transport aircraft', *Asian Defence Journal*, July 1994, p. 82; and 'Malaysia and Indonesia deal in locally built aircraft', *Asian Defence Journal*, Apr. 1995, p. 79.

[33] 'ASEAN countries offered training facilities', *Jane's Defence Weekly*, 29 July 1995, p. 12.

[34] Karniol (note 28).

[35] Karniol, R., '"Cobra Gold" extends ASEAN co-operation', *Jane's Defence Weekly*, 21 May 1994, p. 12.

[36] *The Star* (Petaling Jaya), 18 Jan. 1995, p. 6. On the Nordic battalion, see Karhilo, J., Redesigning Nordic military contributions to multilateral peace operations', *SIPRI Yearbook 1996: Armaments, Disarmament and International Security* (Oxford University Press: Oxford, 1996), appendix 2C, pp. 101–16.

[37] Acharya, A., 'ASEAN–UN cooperation in peace and preventive diplomacy: its contribution to regional security', *Indonesian Quarterly*, vol. 22, no. 3 (1994), pp. 215–26.

view to 'alleviating suspicion and building mutual understanding and confidence'.[38] Viet Nam has established defence links with Indonesia, the Philippines and Thailand. The Philippines has offered training facilities for Vietnamese officers at the Philippine Military Academy and indicated a desire to cooperate on maintenance and reconditioning of defence equipment. Thailand and Viet Nam have agreed 'to exchange military attachés, step up exchanges of commanding officers and regularly share military information'.[39] An offer by Thailand, however, to establish a 'hot line' between Hanoi and Bangkok, exchange equipment and hold bilateral naval exercises has been turned down by Viet Nam pending progress in resolving their overlapping territorial claims in the Gulf of Thailand, which attests to lingering mutual suspicions.[40] A visit by Viet Nam's Defence Minister General Doan Thue to Malaysia in October 1994 covered a Malaysian small-arms factory, the headquarters of the Malaysian Special Forces Regiment and the Lumut Naval Base, suggesting the range of cooperation that might be undertaken in the future.[41]

III. Objectives and functions

Defence cooperation among sovereign states may serve two broad purposes. The first and perhaps most familiar objective is to deter and defend against commonly perceived threats. Threat-oriented defence cooperation usually involves significant inter-operability among the armed forces of the participating states, a joint command and control structure, a high degree of standardization of weapon systems and a formal guarantee of reciprocal assistance against aggression. Such cooperation may be undertaken on a bilateral or multilateral basis, although in the history of the contemporary international system the bilateral type has been more frequent. With few exceptions, developing countries have preferred bilateral defence arrangements with major powers to multilateral alliances among themselves.[42]

---

[38] *Straits Times*, 7 Dec. 1993, p. 14.

[39] Cited in Thayer, C. A., International Institute for Strategic Studies, *Beyond Indochina*, Adelphi Paper no. 297 (Oxford University Press: Oxford, 1995), p. 43.

[40] 'Vietnam comes slowly into the fold', *Jane's Defence Weekly*, 12 Nov. 1994, p. 16.

[41] *New Straits Times*, 20 Oct. 1994, p. 2.

[42] For a conceptual discussion of alternative frameworks for security and defence cooperation in the developing world, see Acharya, A., 'Regional military–security cooperation in the Third World: a conceptual analysis of the Association of Southeast Asian Nations', *Journal of Peace Research*, vol. 29, no. 1 (Jan. 1992), pp. 7–21.

ASEAN member states have generally avoided threat-oriented defence cooperation, although they have entered into such agreements with external powers such as the USA and Australia. As noted above, some of the bilateral security arrangements within ASEAN have been geared to internal rather than external threats.

To be sure, the development of intra-ASEAN bilateral security ties does not preclude collective action against external or internal threats in time of need, even if such cooperation is difficult. Najib Razak, a former Defence Minister of Malaysia, has even claimed that, given the degree of inter-operability achieved among the ASEAN forces as a result of bilateral exercises, 'there is nothing to prevent ASEAN from acting collectively if there is the political will to do so . . . If there is a need to have an ASEAN military force, it could be done almost overnight'.[43] Yet the potential for such collective action remains severely circumscribed by intra-ASEAN suspicions, the lack of a commonly perceived threat to facilitate peacetime planning and problems of coordinating logistics, communications and leadership functions.

A second objective of defence cooperation may be to induce greater transparency and understanding among the participating states. Transparency-oriented defence cooperation is a necessary step in the development of security communities, the main function of which is to reduce the likelihood of military conflict between the participating actors.[44] Such cooperation may include joint exercises, intelligence sharing, high-level visits and officer exchanges, and provision of military education and field training facilities. These types of cooperation also occur within threat-oriented alliances, but, unlike the latter, transparency-oriented defence cooperation involves no advance planning or preparations against common threats. Instead, military links develop between countries which may continue to view each other as potential adversaries in the hope that the resulting dynamic of communication and transparency will reduce the likelihood of war and facilitate crisis management.

A careful look at the history of intra-ASEAN defence cooperation reveals that much of it falls into the second category. This is evident from a statement in 1991 by General Hashim Mohammed Ali, the

---

[43] Karniol, R., 'The Jane's interview', *Jane's Defence Weekly*, 18 Dec. 1993, p. 32.

[44] On the differences between a defence community and a security community, see Acharya, A.,'Association of Southeast Asian Nations: security community or defence community?', *Pacific Affairs*, vol. 64, no. 2 (summer 1991), pp. 159–78.

then Chief of Malaysian Defence Forces, listing the following as the main aims of ASEAN defence and security cooperation: (*a*) to enhance the security of the cooperating members (two or more); (*b*) to contribute to the larger ASEAN security; (*c*) to maximize resources, expertise and technologies and avoid waste; (*d*) to reduce conflicts; (*e*) to provide a mechanism for resolving conflict; and (*f*) to facilitate confidence-building measures.[45]

Of these six goals, none directly relates to threat-oriented cooperation, while the last three clearly fall into the transparency-oriented category.

Against the backdrop of continued tensions, rivalries and suspicions among the members, intra-ASEAN defence relations have been geared primarily to developing the habit of conflict avoidance rather than to preparing against common threats. Bilateral military exercises are thus not directed against any specific external threat but are designed, as Singapore's defence minister once put it, to 'build links with . . . neighbours, overcome suspicions and promote cooperation'.[46]

IV. Problems and prospects

In recent years ASEAN policy makers seem increasingly to have accepted the need for enhanced transparency measures. For example, Singapore's Defence Minister, Yeo Ning Hong, listed 'greater transparency in armaments and arms control measures' as an important task for the ARF.[47] Malaysia's former Defence Minister Najib Razak has specifically called for the creation of a regional arms register.[48] Perhaps the most detailed proposal for such a register was made by the Philippines at the Special ASEAN Senior Officials Meeting held in Bangkok in March 1994. The Philippine proposal envisaged a South-East Asian Register of Conventional Arms and Military Expenditure (RCAME) as 'a confidence-building measure which would promote greater transparency with respect to a nation's inten-

[45] Ali, H. A. (Gen.), 'Prospects for defence and security cooperation in ASEAN', Paper presented to the Conference on ASEAN and the Asia–Pacific Region: Prospects for Security Cooperation in the 1990s, Manila, 5–7 June 1991, p. 3.

[46] 'An exclusive interview with Singapore's Defence Chief [Lt-Gen. Winston Choo, Chief of the General Staff]', *Asian Defence Journal*, no. 3 (1989), p. 46.

[47] Karniol, R., 'The Jane's interview', *Jane's Defence Weekly*, 19 Feb. 1994, p. 52.

[48] Ghosh, N., 'M'sian deterrent capability a positive contribution: Najib', *Business Times* (Singapore), 13 July 1993, p. 3.

tions'. The proposed register is to be modelled after the United Nations Register of Conventional Arms (UNROCA). Its aim, as envisaged in the Philippine proposal, is 'to help ensure that the arms modernization programs of South-East Asian states will not escalate into an arms race'.[49]

Bilateral defence links within ASEAN may be useful tools for greater strategic transparency, but this approach has clear limits. A case in point is a suggestion by Lee Kuan Yew that Malaysia and Singapore should consider opening up their military installations to mutual inspection. It received a cool response from Malaysia, whose Defence Minister, Syed Hamid Albar, stated:

I think there should be more transparency. On our part, we have been transparent in the development of our programmes, especially the acquisitions of our new assets. I think the public announcements we have made are quite sufficient. But opening up of installations for inspections is sensitive. It goes against the grain of military culture, which is quite universal. I think we should keep each other informed of our acquisitions. To me, it will go a long way in building up mutual confidence.[50]

ASEAN has responded to the strategic uncertainties of the post-cold war period by launching an initiative to develop a multilateral security dialogue among the Asia–Pacific countries. At its summit meeting in Singapore in 1993 it decided to bring security issues formally onto its agenda. The first meeting of the ARF in 1994 marked the official beginning of this process.[51] The goals of the ARF include the enhancement of confidence-building and preventive-diplomacy measures, leading eventually to 'elaboration of approaches to conflicts'. The second and third ARF meetings, held in Brunei in August 1995 and in Indonesia in July 1996, saw the adoption of an initial set of transparency-oriented measures, including exchange of annual defence postures on a voluntary basis, increased dialogue on security issues on a bilateral, subregional and regional basis, maintenance of senior-level contacts and exchanges among military institutions, and encouragement of participation of the ARF members in the

---

[49] Agnote, D. B., 'ASEAN members agree to regional arms register concept', Kyodo News Service, 8 Apr. 1994.

[50] Kassim, I., 'Malaysia beefs up armed forces for a new role', Straits Times, 24 July 1994, p. 7.

[51] For background, see Acharya, A., International Institute for Strategic Studies, *A New Regional Order in Southeast Asia: ASEAN in the Post-Cold War Era*, Adelphi Paper no. 279 (Brassey's: Oxford, 1993).

UNROCA.[52] Moreover, greater cooperation among ASEAN states on peacekeeping operations has been proposed, with plans for the establishment of a regional peacekeeping training centre.

Yet the realization of such proposals remains far from certain.[53] Defence cooperation among the ASEAN members will remain constrained by the following factors: (a) intramural rivalry; (b) divergent threat perceptions; (c) a preference for informal mechanisms; (d) a shared culture of secrecy; (e) a desire to avoid provoking potential adversaries; and (f) a sense that existing bilateral mechanisms are adequate to meet the primary goal of greater trust and understanding among ASEAN armed forces. Many of these constraints are relevant in assessing the feasibility of enhanced transparency measures such as a regional arms register or the sharing of defence-related information and data.

In the final analysis, lingering suspicions which have thwarted the development of greater subregional and regional defence cooperation in ASEAN will be evident with respect to the creation of defence-related transparency mechanisms. While ASEAN has accepted the need for security consultations, dialogue and transparency, it cannot be taken for granted that the transition to more formal and multilateral transparency regimes will be made. Individual ASEAN members are likely to reject intrusive measures of transparency as a threat to national security. While some substantive transparency measures within ASEAN cannot be ruled out in the future, they will be feasible only if defined in very broad terms. The aim of the exercise cannot be just to create a formal document, but to launch a gradual and broader process of confidence building consistent with ASEAN's extremely cautious approach to defence and security multilateralism.

[52] Acharya, A., 'ARF's challenges', *Trends* (Singapore), no. 60 (26–27 Aug. 1995), p. 1.

[53] For an assessment of problems facing the ARF, see Acharya, A., 'ASEAN and Asia Pacific multilateralism: managing regional security', eds A. Acharya and R. Stubbs, *New Challenges for ASEAN: Emerging Policy Issues* (University of British Columbia Press: Vancouver, BC, 1995), pp. 182–202.

6. Defining legitimate and unwarranted military acquisitions in South-East Asia

Bates Gill

I. Introduction

Data sharing and transparency in military acquisitions should not consist of simple 'laundry lists'. Such exchanges should serve as the bases for defining and determining what is a 'legitimate' as opposed to an 'unwarranted' weapon acquisition. The acquisition of weapons and their legitimate or unwarranted character present difficult and sensitive issues for debate. Nevertheless, as Syed Hamid Albar, the Defence Minister of Malaysia, has argued, 'A time has come for countries in the region to agree to some understanding on what constitutes excessive, threatening or provocative conventional military capabilities'.[1]

In an effort to contribute to this discussion this chapter first briefly summarizes the basic contextual factors in South-East Asia which weigh for and against the encouragement of debate on legitimate as opposed to unwarranted military acquisitions. Section III presents what appear to be areas of consensus or near-consensus with regard to this debate in South-East Asia and section IV looks ahead to consider various ways to stimulate continued fruitful debate on issues related to the development of national defence capabilities in South-East Asia, including the determination of legitimate and unwarranted weapon acquisitions. Section V presents conclusions.

II. The current context

Within South-East Asia, discussions on the issue of unwarranted versus legitimate military acquisitions have reached limited consensus only on certain weapon types, while the debate continues to grapple with several key conceptual issues. There are two strong arguments why such discussions should go forward.

---

[1] 'Malaysia calls for measures to bar regional arms race', *International Herald Tribune*, 7 Feb. 1996, p. 4.

First, from a strictly self-interested point of view, most states recognize that the unlimited diffusion of arms and military technology is contrary to their interests. This would seem particularly true for smaller states whose defence and techno-industrial capacities cannot keep pace with those of stronger neighbours and who should desire some restraints on growth in military capacities. Unrestrained arms diffusion, especially such as leads to imbalances, not only threatens to generate hostilities but can also undermine financial and commercial confidence in regional stability, which in turn weakens economic prospects. Because governments are both the source and the targets of the arms trade, it follows that they share an interest in developing ways to try to shape and regulate its processes and outcomes.

Second, from a legal perspective, because states in the region have entered into certain international agreements and made public pledges concerning arms trade and proliferation, they should develop national and multilateral capacities to adequately assume the burden of these freely chosen obligations and to monitor the commitments they and other states have made.

However, a number of questions will confront progress in the debate on legitimate and unwarranted weapon acquisitions, and will need to be considered carefully.

First, there is no basic and universally accepted set of principles regarding legitimate and unwarranted military acquisitions—especially with regard to conventional weapons—which can be consistently and practically applied in shaping relations among states. Hence such a debate will be breaking some new ground, particularly as discussions apply to South-East Asia.

Second, legitimate concerns of national self-interest—especially regarding military, commercial and techno-industrial issues—will need to be carefully considered as part of the debate. For South-East Asian countries in the relatively early stages of nation building, the development and protection of the universally recognized right to self-defence are a particularly sensitive issue. In a region which has relatively recently shaken off the bonds of its colonial experience, nationalism and self-interested state sovereignty may constrain tendencies towards collectivism, 'shared sovereignty' and ideas perceived as promoting unwelcome restraints on national capabilities. Commercial and techno-industrial benefits also accrue to the recipients of arms and technologies through offset arrangements or spin-off. In South-East

Asia, these points carry special weight as most countries are seeking to advance indigenous techno-industrial capacity in both defence and civilian sectors. In order to proceed, the debate on legitimate and unwarranted military development must seek to address these issues of national interest.

III. Areas of consensus

Weapons of mass destruction

Asia–Pacific participation in agreements and treaties limiting the development and procurement of certain weapons is shown in table 6.1. It shows that the regional record of consensus on the definition of legitimate and unwarranted development of national military capabilities is rather slim, although there are some positive developments. The table illustrates a strong regional consensus against nuclear weapons and their proliferation. Parties to the Non-Proliferation Treaty (NPT), for example, 'believ[e] that the proliferation of nuclear weapons would seriously enhance the danger of nuclear war' and NPT non-nuclear weapon states agree:

not to receive the transfer from any transferor whatsoever of nuclear weapons or other nuclear explosive devices or of control over such weapons or explosive devices directly, or indirectly; not to manufacture or otherwise acquire nuclear weapons or other nuclear explosive devices and not to seek or receive any assistance in the manufacture of nuclear weapons or other nuclear explosive devices.[2]

Moreover, on 15 December 1995 the 10 states of South-East Asia, recalling the 1971 Declaration on the Zone of Peace, Freedom and Neutrality (ZOPFAN) of 1971 and the subsequent Programme of Action on ZOPFAN of 1993, agreed to the Treaty on the Southeast Asia Nuclear Weapon-Free Zone.[3] The treaty goes beyond NPT obligations in binding the parties not to develop, manufacture or otherwise acquire, possess or have control over nuclear weapons, station or transport nuclear weapons by any means, or test or use nuclear

---

[2] The NPT is reproduced in Kokoski, R., SIPRI, *Technology and the Proliferation of Nuclear Weapons* (Oxford University Press: Oxford, 1995), appendix A, NPT Art. II, p. 256.
[3] The treaty is reproduced in *SIPRI Yearbook 1996: Armaments, Disarmament and International Security* (Oxford University Press: Oxford, 1996), appendix 13A, pp. 601–608.

Table 6.1. Participation by select countries of the Asia–Pacific region in agreements and treaties limiting the development and procurement of certain weapons, as of 1 January 1997

Participant	Geneva Protocol[a]	NPT[b]	Seabed Treaty[c]	BTWC[d]	Inhumane Weapons[e]	CWC[f]	SEA NWFZ[g]
Australia	yes	yes	yes	yes	yes	yes	no
Brunei	no	yes	no	yes	no	yes[s]	yes
Cambodia	yes	yes	no	yes	no	yes[s]	yes[s]
Canada	yes	yes	yes	yes	yes	yes	no
China	yes	yes	yes	yes	yes	yes[s]	no
Indonesia	yes	yes	no	yes	no	yes[s]	yes[s]
Japan	yes	yes	yes	yes	yes	yes	no
Korea, North	yes	yes	no	yes	no	no	no
Korea, South	yes	yes	yes	yes	no	yes[s]	no
Laos	yes	yes	yes	yes	yes	yes[s]	yes
Malaysia	yes	yes	yes	yes	no	yes[s]	yes
Mongolia	yes	yes	yes	yes	yes	yes	no
Myanmar	no	yes	no	yes[s]	no	yes[s]	yes
New Zealand	yes	yes	yes	yes	yes	yes[s]	no
Papua New Guinea	yes	yes	no	yes	no	yes	no
Philippines	yes	yes	yes	yes	yes	yes	yes[s]
Russia	yes	yes	yes	yes	yes	yes[s]	no
Singapore	no	yes	yes	yes	no	yes[s]	yes[s]
Taiwan#	no	yes	no	yes	no	no	no
Thailand	yes	yes	no	yes	no	yes[s]	yes[s]
United States	yes	yes	yes	yes	yes	yes[s]	no
Viet Nam	yes	yes	yes	yes	yes[s]	yes[s]	yes

^a 1925 Protocol for the prohibition of the use in war of asphyxiating, poisonous or other gases, and of bacteriological methods of warfare.

^b 1968 Treaty on the non-proliferation of nuclear weapons.

^c 1971 Treaty on the prohibition of the emplacement of nuclear weapons and other weapons of mass destruction on the seabed and the ocean floor and in the subsoil thereof.

^d 1972 Convention on the prohibition of the development, production and stockpiling of bacteriological (biological) and toxin weapons and on their destruction.

^e 1981 Convention on prohibitions or restrictions on the use of certain conventional weapons which may be deemed to be excessively injurious or to have indiscriminate effects.

^f 1993 Convention on the prohibition of the development, production, stockpiling and use of chemical weapons and on their destruction.

^g Treaty on the Southeast Asia Nuclear Weapon-Free Zone.

[#] Taiwan, while not officially recognized as a sovereign state by most governments, is listed as a party to those agreements which it has signed and ratified.

[¤] Signed but not ratified.

Source: Ferm, R., 'Arms control and disarmament agreements', *SIPRI Yearbook 1997: Armaments, Disarmament and International Security* (Oxford University Press: Oxford, forthcoming 1997), annexe A.

weapons.[4] It also establishes a Commission (at the foreign minister level) to oversee the implementation of the treaty and an Executive Committee (at the senior official level) to ensure proper verification measures in accordance with a 'control system' of information exchanges, requests for clarifications and fact-finding missions as described in the treaty. Both the Commission and the Executive Committee, comprising all the parties to the treaty, will take decisions by consensus or barring that by a two-thirds majority of those present and voting. The treaty also stipulates that the Commission may decide to take 'remedial measures' as appropriate when the Executive Committee determines a breach of the treaty by one of the parties.[5]

With regard to other weapons of mass destruction, parties to the 1972 Biological and Toxin Weapons Convention (BTWC) agree 'never under any circumstances to develop, produce, stockpile or otherwise acquire or retain' microbial or other biological agents other than for peaceful purposes, or their weapons or delivery systems.[6] As to chemical weapons, a number of states in the region are signatories to the 1993 Chemical Weapons Convention (CWC) but only six countries of the region have ratified it (see table 6.1).

Regional participation in international agreements related to conventional weapons, such as the 1981 Inhumane Weapons Convention, is considerably less than participation in agreements related to weapons of mass destruction.

Arms trade and defence policy statements

It also appears that in recent years countries in South-East Asia have come closer to a consensus on the need to consider greater information exchange and transparency on issues related to conventional defence procurement and policies.

At an official level, the idea of arms trade information exchange in ASEAN has gained a certain amount of support. Both Malaysian and Philippine officials have made calls for a register, while the UN

[4] Treaty on the Southeast Asia Nuclear Weapon-Free Zone, in *SIPRI Yearbook 1996* (note 3), Art. 3, pp. 602–603.

[5] On the Commission, the Executive Committee and their respective activities, see Treaty on the Southeast Asia Nuclear Weapon-Free Zone (note 3), Arts 8–14, pp. 603–605.

[6] The BTWC is reproduced in Geissler, E. and Woodall, J. P. (eds), *Control of Dual-Threat Agents: The Vaccines for Peace Programme*, SIPRI Chemical & Biological Warfare Studies no. 15, annexe A, pp. 243–45; see Art. I, p. 243. All the countries of the Asia–Pacific region but Myanmar are full parties to the BTWC (see table 6.1).

Group of Experts noted ARF efforts in this regard and stated that regional organizations could 'address the possible regional security concerns relating to participation in the Register'.[7] Furthermore, at the August 1995 ARF meeting in Brunei, participating ministers agreed: (*a*) to encourage all ARF countries to enhance their dialogues and consultations on political and security cooperation on a bilateral, subregional and regional basis; (*b*) that the ARF countries should submit to the ARF or ARF Senior Officials Meeting, on a voluntary basis, an annual statement of their defence policy; and (*c*) to take note of the increased participation in the United Nations Register of Conventional Arms (UNROCA) since the first ARF and encourage those not yet participating to soon do so.[8]

ARF participation in the UNROCA and ASEAN participation in particular have in fact been quite high, as table 6.2 indicates. In addition, as chapter 7 of this volume notes, the development of defence White Papers in the region, while in its early stages, has moved in a positive direction. These types of participation in transparency and data-sharing programmes are encouraging. However, a regional approach to further refine the concepts and procedures of registers and White Papers is required, particularly to address their present weaknesses. Moreover, the multilateral development of defence procurement information exchanges will contribute to furthering the debate on issues related to legitimate needs and unwarranted development.

Track-two processes

Track-two processes abound in the Asia–Pacific and often focus on security-related concerns. Most recently, some track-two processes have taken up more specific discussions related to defence procurement and policies, which are important steps in constructive dialogue on the broader issue of legitimate needs versus unwarranted develop

---

[7] United Nations, Report on the continuing operation of the United Nations Register of Conventional Arms and its further development, UN document A/49/316, 22 Sep. 1994, para. 39.

[8] 'Chairman's statement of the Second ASEAN Regional Forum (ARF), Aug. 1995, Bandar Seri Begawan', provided to the Northeast Asia Peace and Security Network by the Pacific Forum CSIS, Honolulu.

Table 6.2. Participation in the United Nations Register of Conventional Arms, 1992–94, by participants in the ASEAN Regional Forum

State	1992 Data on imports	Data on exports	Note verbale	Info	1993 Data on imports	Data on exports	Note verbale	Info	1994 Data on imports	Data on exports	Note verbale	Info
Australia	yes	nil	..	yes	yes	nil	..	yes	yes	nil	..	yes
Brunei	no submission recorded				no submission recorded				no submission recorded			
Cambodia	no submission recorded				no submission recorded				no submission recorded			
Canada	yes	yes	..	yes	yes	yes	..	yes	yes	yes	..	yes
China	yes	yes	..	no	nil	yes	..	no	yes	yes	..	no
India	yes	yes	..	no	nil	yes	..	no	yes	nil	..	no
Indonesia	nil	nil	..	no	yes	..	..	no	yes	..	..	no
Japan	yes	nil	..	yes	yes	nil	..	yes	yes	nil	..	yes
Laos	no submission recorded				no submission recorded				no submission recorded			
Malaysia	nil	nil	yes	no	yes	nil	..	no	yes	nil	..	no
Myanmar	no submission recorded				no submission recorded				no submission recorded			
New Zealand	yes	nil	..	yes	yes	nil	..	yes	yes	nil	..	yes
Papua N.G.	nil	nil	..	no	nil	nil	..	no	nil	nil	yes	no
Philippines	yes	nil	yes	no	yes	..	..	no	yes	..	..	no
Russia	nil	yes	..	no	nil	yes	..	no	nil	yes	..	no
Singapore	yes	nil	..	no	yes	nil	..	no	yes	nil	..	no
South Korea	yes	nil	..	yes	yes	yes	..	yes	yes	yes	..	yes
Thailand	no submission recorded				yes	nil	..	no	yes	nil	..	no
United States	yes	yes	yes	yes	yes	yes	yes	yes	yes	yes	yes	yes
Viet Nam	no submission recorded				no submission recorded				nil	nil	..	no

Notes: 'Yes' denotes submission of data and information. For uniform tabulation, 'nil' is used in cases where governments reported using terms such as 'nil', 'no', 'none', a dash ('–'), '0' or otherwise indicated that no exports and/or imports had taken place in the period indicated. An ellipse ('..') indicates that no information was supplied. In some cases, however, an explanation was provided in the note of the country in question. 'Info' denotes background information provided as part of a submission.

The ARF was founded in 1994. The European Union is represented as an organization in the ARF, but the table does not include EU member states. Viet Nam joined the ARF in 1995. India and Myanmar joined the ARF in 1996.

Source: Table based on information available as of 6 Mar. 1996 in United Nations documents A/48/344, A/49/352, and A/50/547, and addenda.

ment. For example, in 1995 SIPRI and MIMA established a research and publication effort to address the issue of defence procurement, transparency and security in South-East Asia. The project involves experts drawn from the region and around the world and has held regional workshops for officials and analysts and published extensive analysis and documentation, including a de facto arms trade register of conventional arms for ASEAN.[9]

Another leading effort is the work under the auspices of the Working Group on Confidence- and Security-Building Measures of the Council for Security Cooperation in the Asia Pacific (CSCAP). In workshop-style meetings in May 1995, April 1996 and November 1996, this group brought specific focus to issues of military transparency, the pros and cons of a regional arms register along the lines of the UNROCA and the development of defence White Papers in the region. This effort has resulted in the presentation and publication of valuable research and proposals on these issues.[10]

The UN has made important contributions to generating debate on these issues in the official and track-two communities. At the Eighth Regional Disarmament Meeting in the Asia–Pacific Region, held in Kathmandu in early 1996, the UNCDA sponsored a one-day workshop on the Asia–Pacific experience with the UNROCA which brought together both officials and researchers to address the past and future prospects of the UN Register, Asia–Pacific participation, and possible approaches to and variants of the UN Register at a regional level.

IV. Points of departure

The following discussion serves as a catalyst for further debate on legitimate versus unwarranted military capabilities in South-East Asia. In the end such discussions need to be carried out by those most

---

[9] Publications of the project include Gill, B., Mak, J. N. and Wezeman, S. T., *ASEAN Arms Acquisitions: Developing Transparency* (MIMA: Kuala Lumpur, 1995); Wezeman, S. T., *East Asian Maritime Arms Acquisitions: A Database of East Asian Naval Arms Imports and Production 1975–1996* (MIMA: Kuala Lumpur, forthcoming 1997); and the present volume.

[10] Publications related to the CSBM Working Group include Cossa, R. A. (ed.), *Promoting Regional Transparency: Defense Policy Papers and the United Nations Register of Conventional Arms* (Pacific Forum CSIS: Honolulu, July 1996); Cossa, R. A. (ed.), *Asia Pacific Confidence and Security Building Measures* (Center for Strategic and International Studies: Washington, DC, 1995); and Cossa, R. A. (ed.), *Toward a Regional Arms Register in the Asia Pacific* (Pacific Forum CSIS: Honolulu, Aug. 1995).

closely concerned and with the region-specific nature of the discussions kept firmly in mind.

Unwarranted development

Conditions which enhance the offensive or destabilizing character of weapons deserve special attention. David Mussington and John Sislin find that instability and conflict are most likely when arms acquisitions by their nature (*a*) result in decreased warning time, (*b*) give on country 'breakthrough' capabilities, (*c*) lead to a broadening of target sets, (*d*) permit no effective countermeasures, (*e*) give one side better information concerning another's military preparations, and (*f*) create hostility.[11] Using these parameters, the acquisition of such capabilities as aircraft-carriers, long-range cruise missiles, certain modern anti-ship missiles, at-sea replenishment and in-flight refuelling, attack aircraft, precision-guided weapons, combined-arms and amphibious assault training, and large modern submarine fleets might be deemed unwarranted in certain South-East Asian contexts.

Two caveats should be stated. First, the simple possession of certain weapons does not necessarily lead to offensive action. Rather, the political, military and geo-strategic contexts within which these capabilities operate affect the offensive character of the weapons in question. For example, the offensive character of the weapon systems noted above could become more pronounced in a deteriorating political situation in which one or both sides in a dispute perceived a military advantage in striking first.

Second, most military forces in South-East Asia are not structured, armed or doctrinally prepared to carry out significant offensive operations against neighbouring countries but are mostly defensive in character. Those arsenals in South-East Asia which include anti-ship missiles (AShMs), air-to-surface missiles (ASMs) and advanced strike aircraft can pose a limited threat, especially with regard to the disrup-

---

[11] Mussington, D. and Sislin, J., 'Defining destabilizing arms acquisitions', *Jane's Intelligence Review*, vol. 17, no. 2 (Feb. 1995), pp. 88–90. Similarly, Ross Babbage argues that focus should be brought to 8 criteria in considering legitimate defence development: the offensive or defensive nature of a weapon; scale of acquisitions; speed of acquisition; use and deployment of a weapon; international political conditions; the past record of international behaviour of a recipient; the openness of the recipient's political system; and the involvement of the recipient in CSBMs. Babbage, R., 'Enhancing national military capabilities in the Asia Pacific region: legitimate needs versus unwarranted development', Paper presented at the Tenth Asia–Pacific Roundtable, Kuala Lumpur, 5–8 June 1996.

tion of naval and commercial shipping, but much of this offensive capacity can be countered by defences in the region, which reduces the likely success of offensive operations, especially against land-based, strategically important sites.

However, this situation could change with certain acquisitions planned for the future. For example, the increased capacity and number of strike aircraft which give one country an overwhelming advantage and sense of invulnerability could lead to offensive operations, either by the possessor country or by one of its neighbours acting to decisively neutralize the newly developed advantage of its better-armed counterpart. Similarly, the acquisition of technologies which give greater 'reach' or improved sensory capabilities could also tip the scales in a way which leads to offensive action. Desmond Ball points to certain offensive acquisitions in the region—maritime strike aircraft, modern surface combatants, submarines and long-range anti-ship missiles—as a cause for concern, particularly as they contribute to 'reach', surprise, opacity, uncertainty and miscalculation.[12]

Legitimate acquisitions

Systems which might be considered legitimate or stabilizing in South-East Asia might include land-based anti-air and limited anti-ship capabilities, coastal defence navies and early-warning systems which discourage offensive surprise by a would-be attacker. One researcher has developed a model of 'defensive deterrence' for navies intent on maintaining coastal defence and policing of EEZs.[13] According to this model, a defensive navy would include: (a) off-shore patrol vessels for use in EEZs armed with 75-mm and 20-mm guns, an unarmed helicopter (possibly small anti-ship missiles) and anti-air defence missiles; (b) shallow-water mines and coastal mine-laying ships; (c) land-based mobile anti-ship missiles with a range of no more than 50 km; (d) helicopters armed with short-range anti-ship missiles and with anti-submarine detection and warfare capabilities; (e) unarmed surveillance aircraft; and (f) land-based fighter aircraft with anti-air

---

[12] Ball, D., *Trends in Military Acquisitions in the Asia-Pacific Region: Implications for Security and Prospects for Constraints and Controls*, Working Paper no. 273 (Australian National University, Strategic and Defence Studies Centre: Canberra, 1993), pp. 20–21.

[13] Grove, E., 'Naval technology and stability', eds W. A. Smit, J. Grin and L. Voronkov, *Military Technological Innovation and Stability in a Changing World* (VU University Press: Amsterdam, 1992), pp. 202–203.

systems. An adjusted alternative similar to these deployments—perhaps limiting mine usage in maritime-dependent South-East Asia—might be well suited to the South-East Asian context, especially as these states do not have the need for long-range operations. These parameters may serve as a kind of model to stimulate further debate and encourage consensus as to what might constitute legitimate or unwarranted military acquisitions.

Another way of mitigating the offensive nature of relatively large naval fleets is to incorporate them into multinational forces for peacekeeping or policing duties. This is a far-off development for ASEAN, if it happens at all. However, continued stable political conditions and the enormous technological and operational expense of modern navies may combine to make this option increasingly feasible for the future.

A model to identify weapons of concern

The determination of offensive and defensive capacity requires an understanding of the specific missions, roles and strategies to be performed by a given military and its equipment.[14] Thus, discussions in South-East Asia on legitimate as opposed to unwarranted military acquisitions might begin by addressing these issues as shown in the simple model in tables 6.3, 6.4 and 6.5. These three tables together present a three-part method of defining maritime missions and corresponding acquisitions in South-East Asia. By identifying specific missions for certain countries, the model suggests which acquisitions are best suited for those missions—that is, which acquisitions might be considered legitimate or unwarranted.

Table 6.3 sets out five specific maritime defence missions. In table 6.4 the model suggests which countries in the region would need to perform these missions as part of their defence requirements. Table 6.5 suggests which acquisitions best correlate with which mission requirements. For example, in the case of Brunei, those acquisitions which correlate to its mission requirements related to defence, surveillance and the Spratly Islands would be deemed legitimate objectives. Acquisitions which correlate to other missions—protection of sea lines of communication (SLOC) or power projection, for example—might be deemed unwarranted. It is clear that some

---

[14] Russ Swinnerton developed these arguments at the MIMA–SIPRI Workshop on ASEAN Arms Trade Transparency, Kuala Lumpur, 3 Oct. 1995.

Table 6.3. Maritime defence missions in South-East Asia

Mission	Description
Defence	Defence of territory and contiguous waters, including sea assertion and denial. In the absence of a specific threat can justify a range of acquisitions
Surveillance	Surveillance and patrol of EEZs, including sea assertion; requires lower-order surveillance, patrol and response. Has become more prominent following conclusion of the UNCLOS
SLOC	SLOC and archipelagic waters control and protection. Particularly important for Indonesia and the Philippines but also for Malaysia
Spratlys	Protection of sovereignty, including maritime and air defence and strike capabilities for credibility and deterrence purposes. Applies to all claimants to the Spratlys
Power projection	Strategic surveillance and strike capabilities; capabilities required for this mission can be used in performing other missions; evidence of planning to perform this mission may destabilize regional security

Table 6.4. South-East Asian maritime defence missions by country

	Mission				
Country	Defence	Surveillance	SLOC	Spratlys	Power
Brunei	yes	yes	no	yes	no
Cambodia	yes	yes	no	no	no
Indonesia	yes	yes	yes	no	no
Laos	no	no	no	no	no
Malaysia	yes	yes	yes	yes	no
Myanmar	yes	yes	no	no	no
Philippines	yes	yes	yes	yes	no
Singapore	yes	yes	yes	no	no
Thailand	yes	yes	no	no	no
Viet Nam	yes	yes	no	yes	no

capabilities—such as frigates—which might serve for power projection are also legitimate for protecting SLOC. Further discussion by interested parties would be necessary to clarify the intended mission of a given acquisition.

Table 6.5. Legitimate acquisitions for given missions in South-East Asia

	Mission				
Acquisition	Defence	Surveillance	SLOC	Spratlys	Power
Naval vessels					
Aircraft carrier	no	no	no	no	yes
Frigate	yes	no	yes	yes	yes
Corvette	yes	yes	yes	yes	yes
MCM	yes	no	yes	yes	yes
OPV	yes	yes	no	yes	yes
Missile FAC	yes	no	yes	no	no
Submarine	yes	no	yes	yes	yes
Underway logistics	no	no	no	no	yes
Aircraft					
Fighter/strike	yes	no	yes	yes	yes
Helicopter	yes	yes	yes	yes	yes
Maritime patrol	yes	yes	yes	yes	yes

Notes: MCM = mine countermeasure ships; OPV = offshore patrol vessels; FAC = fast attack craft.

Source of tables 6.3–6.5: Based on Swinnerton, R., 'Maritime security and the geostrategic imperatives of ASEAN in the 1990s', Working paper submitted to the SIPRI–MIMA Project on Arms Trade Transparency in South-East Asia, Mar. 1996.

In the absence of clear and universal principles concerning illegitimate weapons in the region (with the exception, perhaps, of weapons of mass destruction), the debate must begin to take into account the scenarios, contexts and missions in which certain weapons might be deployed and used. The model focuses attention on those systems which might be considered unnecessary under certain mission circumstances and provides some basic points of departure for discussions on legitimate needs as opposed to unwarranted acquisitions.

V. Conclusions

At this early stage, discussions of legitimate and unwarranted acquisitions must realistically recognize the scope of their contribution to stability. This contribution lies initially in creating consensus, promoting confidence and strengthening political relationships, thereby reducing perceived needs for weapons—offensive or defensive, legitimate or otherwise.

Moreover, as military technology outpaces the processes of diplomacy, achieving a reasonably effective arms-related transparency and data-sharing structure may be difficult. Here again, the process of discussion and debate—as opposed to the end itself—can positively contribute to stable political conditions. Hence, discussions on legitimate versus unwarranted military acquisitions should start sooner rather than later, and can be part of the broader process of security and confidence building in the region.

7. Development of defence White Papers in the Asia–Pacific region

Kang Choi and Panitan Wattanayagorn

I. Introduction

In the Asia–Pacific region the number of countries publishing a defence White Paper is increasing and many countries that do not at present publish one are planning to do so soon.[1] Overall, this trend indicates an increased appreciation among countries in the region of the need for greater openness and transparency on defence-related issues. This is consistent with policies generated at the regional level, such as the statement issued by the ministers gathered for the ARF in August 1995. This statement, in part, called on 'the ARF countries to submit to the ARF or ARF-SOM [ARF Senior Officials Meeting], on a voluntary basis, an annual statement of their defence policy'.[2]

Currently, the form and content of defence White Papers differ from one country to another, and the type, scope and level of information vary widely. In some cases a current version of a country's defence White Paper differs in form and content from those previously published. Each state will, of course, continue to determine the form, contents, scope and level of information. Nevertheless, a widely accepted consensus on what a defence White Paper ought to look like might help to reduce such variations and to increase trust and confidence among the Asia–Pacific nations by reducing the likelihood of misjudgement and misinterpretation. While a standardized, common form is not a likely prospect in the short term, movement towards consensus on a model form for White Papers might improve the overall quality of the information provided.

---

[1] Asia–Pacific countries which have issued defence White Papers or defence policy publications include: Australia, Canada, China, Indonesia, Japan, New Zealand, Singapore, South Korea, Thailand and the United States. Some countries—Australia, Canada, New Zealand, Japan, Singapore, South Korea and the United States—have issued such publications for a number of years. Others in the region—China, Indonesia and Thailand—have begun to issue defence policy papers since the mid-1990s.

[2] 'Chairman's statement of the Second ASEAN Regional Forum (ARF), Aug. 1995, Bandar Seri Begawan', provided to the Northeast Asia Peace and Security Network by the Pacific Forum CSIS, Honolulu.

This chapter begins by considering the definition and functions of defence White Papers and setting out some standards for their evaluation. It then summarizes several of the current defence White Papers available in the region and includes a more focused case study of the development and publication of that of Thailand, an ASEAN member which began to issue a White Paper in 1994. In conclusion the chapter offers some observations and recommendations about the future development of defence White Papers in the Asia–Pacific region.

II. Definition, function and evaluation

Definition and function

A defence White Paper is an authoritative, publicly available, official statement of policy prepared and published by the agency responsible for defence in a given country and offers a comprehensive description of defence-related issues pertinent to the country. As the highest authoritative government document on defence, a White Paper is a distinctive way of expressing a country's assessment of its security environment, its capability to accomplish national security objectives and its strategies for reacting to perceived national security threats.

Such documents have various functions. First, defence White Papers function within the domestic bureaùcratic and political environments to promote debate, develop consensus and justify policies on security- and defence-related priorities. Government agencies compete for limited resources, and the assessment of the current security environment and threats and expectations for the future provided by a defence White Paper helps government agencies to overcome their differences and reach consensus on policy priorities and resource allocation. They help defence-related agencies promote and justify their goals and budgetary needs and can provide guidance concerning national security objectives to the subordinate service branches. On the basis of the objectives and guidelines outlined, each service branch can identify its own areas of concern and formulate its missions and tasks accordingly.

Second, a properly developed defence White Paper functions as an important confidence- and security-building instrument by offering information which has both a deterrent and a reassuring effect. By suggesting the level of a country's readiness, it informs that country's neighbours, including potential adversaries, of its military capabilities.

At the same time, by offering greater transparency in defence-related affairs it may reassure a country's neighbours as to its security concerns, its strategic intentions and its military capabilities.

A defence White Paper is not intended to achieve complete transparency, largely because revealing too much information could undermine a country's defence or deterrence posture. On the other hand, too much secrecy may increase suspicion and exacerbate the security dilemma between states. Knowing other nations' defence policies helps countries formulate and adjust their own policies accordingly. Without such knowledge, governments tend to formulate and implement defence policies based on worst-case assumptions and unilateral, sometimes biased, interpretation. This can lead to a vicious circle of misperception. By reducing uncertainty, defence White Papers can make it easier for states to identify where, how and to what degree they can cooperate and coordinate their respective defence policies.

These points suggest some of the benefits of regularly publishing a defence White Paper. Whether and how to publish one is a decision to be taken by individual countries. However, the increased numbers of White Papers in the Asia–Pacific region suggest that more countries are finding ways to gain the benefits of transparency while protecting legitimate national interests.

Evaluation

Defence White Papers can be evaluated by at least five criteria: comprehensiveness of contents; balance and mutual supportiveness among different sections of the report; precision and reliability of information; consistency and standardization; and availability.

In order to provide a clear and precise understanding of a nation's defence policy, a defence White Paper should be comprehensive. All relevant areas of national defence—including threat assessment, military requirements, resource allocation, the organization of the military establishment, the maintenance and operation of forces, and the use of force—should be included. Intentional or unintentional omission of certain elements of defence policy is likely to increase suspicion and reduce the quality of the document.

Since a defence White Paper is a comprehensive, internationally circulated information source, its contents should be well-balanced, logically consistent and mutually supportive. It should not deal with certain areas of defence in detail while skipping others, exaggerate minor issues, or be too subjective or full of euphemisms. Subjects, chapters or sections must be logically connected and mutually consistent so that it is possible to understand current defence policies and make reasonable predictions about the future. If possible, information should be backed up by quantitative data. Data on military holdings, arms transfers, defence budgets and manpower are available from international sources such as *The Military Balance*, the *SIPRI Yearbook* chapters on world military expenditure and the arms trade, and the United Nations Register of Conventional Arms (UNROCA). States can use these data or provide their own. For example, submissions made voluntarily to the UNROCA—which is open-source information—could also be included in a country's defence White Paper to allow for further dissemination. Standardization of the framework and of the arrangement of contents of the White Paper is necessary to maintain consistency over the years and ease comparison over time. While some changes in form and content are unavoidable, constant and significant changes to the format of a defence White Paper are likely to undermine its value and reliability.

Finally, a defence White Paper should be publicly available. Otherwise it does not perform its informative function. Each government should provide sufficient copies and improve the accessibility and availability of its White Paper, both at home and abroad.

On the basis of these five criteria, this chapter suggests a model form for a defence White Paper. It should cover at least six categories: threat assessment (or assessment of security environment); national security objectives and goals; current defence posture; defence requirements and initiatives; defence management; and overall evaluation. In addition to these categories, each state should add appendices which may include reference materials, statistical data, an organizational chart of the armed forces and chronologies to add clarity. To make the document more readily accessible at home and abroad, a country should consider the possibility of publishing the defence White Paper in both the official national language and English. A model form for a defence White Paper is shown in table 7.1.

Table 7.1. A model form for a defence White Paper

Principal sections	Subsections
PART I:	
Threat assessment/security environment	International, regional, national
Major areas of concern	International, regional, national
PART II:	
National security objectives	Strategic, tactical
General defence policy approach	Strategic, tactical
PART III:	
Current and future defence posture	Size of force, structure of force, military holdings, use of force, training and exercises, force maintenance, alliances and international military agreements
PART IV:	
Defence requirements	Procurement, military-related research, development and production
PART V:	
Defence management	Planning, personnel, organization, logistics, defence budget
PART VI:	
Overall evaluation/conclusion	
PART VII:	
Appendices and reference materials	

III. Summary of Asia–Pacific defence White Papers

To provide a sense of the different approaches to defence White Papers in the region, this section offers brief summaries and evaluations of such publications by seven countries: Australia, China, Japan, South Korea, New Zealand, Singapore and the USA. Section IV focuses specifically on the development and contents of Thailand's defence White Paper. The descriptions here are neither detailed nor comprehensive but are intended to provide a basic comparison.[3]

[3] Other countries in the region have issued publications which are similar to defence White Papers, including *The Policy of the State Defence and Security of the Republic of Indonesia* (Ministry of Defence and Security: Jakarta, Oct. 1995); and Dato Nordin Yusof and Addul Razak Abdullah Baginda, *Honour and Sacrifice: The Malaysian Armed Forces* (Ministry of Defence: Kuala Lumpur, 1994). Others in the region—such as the Philippines and Viet Nam—are contemplating the publication of defence White Papers or similar statements. Chalmers, M., *Confidence-Building in Southeast Asia*, Bradford Arms Register Series no. 6 (Westview Press: Boulder, Colo., 1996), pp. 221–22.

Australia does not publish its formal defence White Paper regularly but whenever it thinks it necessary and suitable. Its first was published in 1976, the second in 1987 and the third in 1994. The title is *Defending Australia: Defence White Paper* and its contents include: (*a*) foundations of defence policy; (*b*) capabilities for the defence of Australia; (*c*) international defence interests; (*d*) national defence support; (*e*) funding the defence effort; and (*f*) a summary.[4] *Defending Australia* is fairly comprehensive and sets out the basic lines of Australian defence policy on a long-term basis. Australia also updates its near- and mid-term defence policy by preparing and publishing the *Strategic Review,* the *Defence Corporate Plan* and the very detailed *Defence Annual Report* to provide hard data on capabilities, management, budget, performance and achievement in the defence field. By publishing three different defence policy papers, Australia provides very comprehensive, precise, reliable and consistent information on its defence policy.

In November 1995, China published a 34-page document entitled *China: Arms Control and Disarmament.* It includes chapters on: (*a*) promoting peace and development for all mankind; (*b*) reductions in military personnel by one million; (*c*) maintaining a low level of defence spending; (*d*) peaceful uses for military industrial technologies; (*e*) strict control over the transfer of sensitive materials and military equipment; (*f*) active promotion of international arms control and disarmament; and (*g*) concluding remarks.[5] It focuses clearly on arms control and disarmament but chapters 2, 3 and 4 also contain data on force size, structure, equipment, facilities, military expenditure and defence conversion. The information provided is relatively limited and not sufficient to provide a complete picture of Chinese defence policy. Nevertheless, the publication of a defence White Paper has a very important symbolic meaning because it shows that the Chinese leadership and defence establishment are willing to offer and possibly institutionalize a more open channel of communication.[6]

Japan published its first defence White Paper, *Defense of Japan,* in 1970 and the second in 1976, and since then has published a White

---

[4] *Defending Australia: Defence White Paper 1994* (Australian Government Publishing Service: Canberra, 1994).

[5] *China: Arms Control and Disarmament* (Information Office of the State Council of the People's Republic of China: Beijing, 1995).

[6] Discussions held by one of the editors of this volume with Chinese military officials and other security specialists in China in late 1996 suggest that a second White Paper is in preparation and may appear in 1997.

Paper annually. In March 1978, the Defense Agency of Japan set up basic guidelines for the defence White Paper which have been followed since then. The White Paper is divided into two main parts: the text and reference material and statistical data. The text consists of four main chapters, each with several sections. The main chapters in 1995 were: (*a*) the international military situation; (*b*) Japan's defence policy and the present situation of the Self-Defense Forces; (*c*) future issues; and (*d*) the Japanese Self-Defense Forces and society.[7]

Defense of Japan is comprehensive, precise, reliable, balanced and consistent. For example, the 1995 edition was over 360 pages long and provided more than 50 explanatory boxes, diagrams and tables, plus over 70 detailed reference notes in an appendix. The inclusion of reference material and statistical data distinguishes Japan's White Paper from others and enhances its reliability and openness.

South Korea has published the annual *Defense White Paper* since 1988. Like *Defense of Japan* it has five main parts, with two to five chapters in each. The main parts are: (*a*) an overview; (*b*) security environment and threat assessment; (*c*) national defence posture; (*d*) defence management; and (*e*) the people and the military. The White Paper also includes a section with documentation and reference materials.[8] It has maintained the same format since 1988 and, at around 250 pages with more than 40 tables and figures, is quite comprehensive and informative. On the other hand, it lacks balance in that it emphasizes threat assessment and national defence posture while not providing enough information on defence management and procurement. However, it may be natural for South Korea to refrain from releasing certain information because of its particular security environment. With increasing self-confidence in its national defence, it is expected to provide more precise and reliable hard data.

New Zealand's defence White Paper is *The Defence of New Zealand: A Policy Paper*. The most recent edition was published in 1991 and included: (*a*) preface; (*b*) summary; (*c*) introduction; (*d*) the strategic situation; (*e*) New Zealand's security interests; (*f*) defence strategy; (*g*) capabilities needed; (*h*) present force structure; (*i*) planning and funding; (*j*) the way ahead; (*k*) the New Zealand Defence Force (annex 1); (*l*) tasks and sub-tasks (annex 2); and (*m*) diagrams.[9]

---

[7] *Defense of Japan 1995* (Defense Agency of Japan: Tokyo, 1995).
[8] *Defense White Paper 1995–1996* (Ministry of National Defense: Seoul, 1995).
[9] *The Defence of New Zealand 1991: A Policy Paper* (Government Printing Ltd. Wellington, 1991), p. 14.

New Zealand also publishes the *New Zealand Defence Force Annual Report*, which offers very detailed financial reporting, performance assessments and other organizational and administrative information. In addition, the 1990 Defence Act requires the Secretary of Defence, in consultation with the Chief of Defence Force, to submit a *Defence Assessment* to the Prime Minister occasionally. This is prepared jointly by the Ministry of Defence and the New Zealand Defence Force and approved by the Defence Policy Board. Finally, the ministry also issues an annual *Corporate Plan* which describes the organizational roles and financial performance of the Ministry of Defence and the New Zealand Defence Force. Taken together, these publications offer some of the most comprehensive and detailed publicly available information on defence issued by any country.

Since 1990, Singapore has published a biennial defence White Paper entitled *Defence of Singapore*. Its fourth edition was expected to be published in late 1996. Its contents include: (*a*) Singapore's defence and security policies; (*b*) the Singapore Armed Forces and Ministry of Defence; (*c*) citizen soldiers; (*d*) the Army; (*e*) the Air Force; (*f*) the Navy; (*g*) defence technology; (*h*) 'making the best use of what we have'; (*i*) overseas training; and (*j*) future directions.[10] The White Paper covers most areas of national defence, presents Singapore's major concerns and clearly illustrates the command structure of the armed forces. However, it does not have hard data on capabilities. Some data are provided but they are scattered.

The US Department of Defense publishes a defence White Paper in its *Annual Report to the President and the Congress*.[11] In addition, the USA periodically publishes other relevant materials such as the *National Security Strategy of the United States*, a series of strategy reports including the *East Asia Strategy Initiatives* and the *East Asia Strategy Report*, the *Bottom–Up Review* and *Defense Guidance*. Together these publications provide a very comprehensive picture of US national defence policy. The contents of the *Annual Report* itself are comprehensive and the information precise and reliable.

Several observations can be drawn from this review of defence White Papers in the Asia–Pacific region. First, an increasing number of countries in the region publish a defence White Paper or defence policy statement, or are expected to do so in the near future. Second,

[10] *Defence of Singapore 1994* (Ministry of Defence: Singapore, 1994).
[11] US Secretary of Defense, *Annual Report to the President and the Congress 1996* (US Government Printing Office: Washington, DC, 1996).

while they differ in content, form and structure, all these defence White Papers include an assessment of threat and security environment and identify national defence objectives. Third, they vary as to whether they provide information on defence posture and management and in the precision and reliability of the information they provide. Fourth, as each society becomes more open, pluralized, self-confident and economically developed, its defence White Paper becomes more sophisticated and tends to contain more reliable, extensive and precise information backed up by hard data. Publication of a defence White Paper, its degree of reliability and precision, and its scope and comprehensiveness can be regarded as manifestations of national self-confidence, pluralization and development.

IV. The case of Thailand

Process and purpose

While Thailand's security policy has been articulated by a number of Thai élites in the past,[12] its defence policies and concepts of national interests were first formally and systematically described in *The Defence of Thailand 1994*.[13] This was followed by a second edition, *The Defence of Thailand 1996*.

Preparation of the first White Paper was initiated by the Supreme Commander in 1993.[14] A committee of military and government officials, academics and civilians was created to draft the first version. Defence White Papers of several countries, including Australia, Japan, the UK and the USA, were studied and debated in the preparatory stage. After the committee completed the first draft version, it was submitted to a 'defence of Thailand seminar' in 1993 and debated openly among 100 representatives from government and the civilian sector, including the business community. The seminar participants made significant suggestions and certain revisions were incorporated. The revised draft version was then sent to the Supreme Commander

[12] Alagappa, M., *The National Security of Developing States* (Auburn House: Lexington, Mass., 1987), pp. 32–39.

[13] *The Defence of Thailand 1994* (Strategic Research Institute, National Institute of Defence Studies: Bangkok, May 1994).

[14] 'The making of Thailand's defence White Paper', Paper prepared by Strategic Research Institute, National Institute of Defence Studies, Supreme Command Headquarters, for the Asia–Pacific Security Meeting, Bangkok, 21–22 Mar. 1996.

for final approval, and the White Paper was published in May 1994. The process for producing the 1996 White Paper was similar.

The process of producing these White Papers was unprecedented in Thai domestic politics as the military sought direct input from civilians and the private sector in the development and publication of defence concepts and aims. Moreover, debates on such sensitive issues as security requirements and defence budgeting were conducted in an open and civil manner throughout. The entire process reflected a considerably more open atmosphere for defence planning in Thailand than existed previously.

In a postscript, the authors of *The Defence of Thailand 1994* wrote that the changes of the post-cold war period at both the international and the domestic levels had resulted in a 'greater desire by the public to be better informed'. Being better informed, the White Paper continues, 'will result in the most desired situation in a democratic society: a concerned citizenship participating in national affairs and government officials aware of their responsibilities to the people'. Taking note of the confidence-building function of defence White Papers, the authors concluded:

In addition to being of domestic benefit, it is hoped that *The Defence of Thailand 1994* will foster better understanding with countries in the region. War and disputes have been brought about many times by suspicion and mutual distrust. These factors will cause an unending race for arms supremacy, which in turn will be a useless waste of resources that could be used for development in other fields. It is hoped that *The Defence of Thailand 1994* . . . will play a part in promoting friendship among nations in this region of the world.[15]

Description and analysis

The Defence of Thailand 1994 had four main chapters: (*a*) global and regional security situations; (*b*) fundamentals of national strategy; (*c*) the protection of national interests; and (*d*) the Royal Thai Armed Forces in the future. It attempts to address security concerns in a very broad sense, encompassing all levels and aspects of politics, economics and socio-cultural issues. This first White Paper emphasizes the need to defend Thailand's independence, sovereignty and territorial integrity and is concerned with Thailand's position in the inter-

[15] *The Defence of Thailand 1994* (note 13), pp. 73–74.

national arena. It also focuses on internal conditions because Thai leaders are often occupied by the question how they can effectively deal with political crises, pressing economic problems and other critical social issues which influence domestic security.

The Defence of Thailand 1996 follows essentially the same concepts as the 1994 White Paper, but in five chapters: (*a*) global and regional security situations; (*b*) national defence policy; (*c*) protection of national interests and the role of the armed forces; (*d*) national development and civic action; and (*e*) the Royal Thai Armed Forces in the future. Thailand's regional security concerns are more clearly delineated than in the 1994 White Paper, with specific consideration of conditions on the Korean Peninsula and in Cambodia, Myanmar and the South China Sea. Less emphasis is placed on domestic problems, perhaps because government leaders and senior military élites felt that the first White Paper contained too much discussion of them.

In a significant shift from the first defence White Paper, the 1996 version offers greater detail on the role of the military. In addition to new activities such as military-related cooperation with the UN and regional countries, it specifically addresses the role of the armed forces in domestic affairs. The chapter on national development and civic action describes military activities including implementing projects initiated by the royal family, creating national unity, participating in solving economic and social problems, developing human resources, assisting civic affairs and providing disaster relief.

The 1996 White Paper also includes more detailed breakdowns of military expenditure, comparisons between the defence budget and other government outlays, and figures showing defence expenditure as a proportion of central government expenditure and gross domestic product. While this additional information can be obtained from the parliament, the Budget Bureau and other open sources, its provision in the White Paper suggests that the Thai military is beginning to feel more confident in disclosing defence expenditure figures more openly.

Thailand's defence White Papers tend to define security broadly, understanding it as a comprehensive and multidimensional concept encompassing social well-being, good citizenship and economic prosperity. Traditional conceptions and aspects of security and defence— such as threats, deterrence and orders of battle—are not emphasized as much. The articulation of defence policy is mostly in the abstract and is very loosely structured in the first two White Papers. The first White Paper, while produced by the Ministry of Defence, actually sets out broad issues and goals which are well beyond the capability of any single government entity to address fully. In addition, statements on security concerns and priorities are not well supported by indicators such as military spending and arms procurement. However, an attempt to improve this deficiency emerges in the second White Paper.

More importantly, the military is not the only barrier to greater detail and coherence. The Thai Parliament also places certain limitations on the transparency of White Papers. Further progress towards greater comprehensiveness and coherence for Thai White Papers will probably require significant changes in circles outside the military.

V. Conclusions

Several conclusions and suggestions may be drawn from this review of the development of defence White Papers in the Asia–Pacific region. First, while the number of states issuing defence White Papers or similar documents is on the rise, the publications vary considerably as to comprehensiveness, balance, precision and reliability, consistency and standardization, and availability. Hence their value in serving information, bureaucratic and confidence- and security-building functions also varies. Second, the diversity among the region's defence White Papers may reflect the relative degrees of national self-confidence, pluralization and development in the countries of the Asia–Pacific region. As they become more confident, pluralized and developed, the general value and reliability of defence White Papers in the region are likely to improve.

For the time being, it is not realistic to expect all countries in the region to produce a White Paper similar to the model in table 7.1. Movement in this direction will take time and will require consensus on a number of difficult issues.

First, widespread consensus on the merits of defence White Papers will be necessary. Fortunately, evidence suggests that this sort of consensus is already emerging in the Asia–Pacific region. The expressed support of the ARF and the evident increase in the number of countries in the region contemplating or publishing defence White Papers are encouraging indicators.

Second, once consensus on the value of publishing defence White Papers is firmly established, countries might consider discussing ways to remedy the problems caused by the wide variation in the quantity and quality of information supplied by different White Papers. One approach would be to build consensus on the value of establishing a standard model for countries to follow. Such a model White Paper would not necessarily be a template for all countries to follow but would set general standards to which countries could agree to refer when preparing their White Papers. Debate and discussion among concerned experts could help generate such a vision of an ideal model.

The third phase of this process would involve getting governments to accept elements of the ideal White Paper as generally accepted standards for what White Papers ought to include. Such broadly accepted standards would help improve each country's White Paper in terms of the five criteria mentioned above: comprehensiveness, balance, precision and reliability, consistency and standardization, and availability. However, for practical reasons, pushing for rapid integration of all five criteria into a broadly accepted model White Paper is not realistic in the short term. It may even prove counter-productive, making countries more reluctant to move in the direction of building up a commonly shared model paper.

A step-by-step approach towards building consensus on a standard form for defence White Papers would be most suitable at this stage. Rather than seeking simultaneously and fully to meet all five criteria, the general model for White Papers should be gradually built up over time. It seems more reasonable to start by emphasizing comprehensiveness and availability. Both these criteria are fundamental to the objectives of a defence White Paper and countries may therefore have less difficulty reaching consensus on their value. Countries could be encouraged to agree that all defence White Papers should be comprehensive enough to cover the key areas of defence policy: perception, orientation and capability. Countries may agree to cover each of the sections suggested in table 7.1, or, if this turns out to be too difficult politically, parts I, II and VI might be more easily encouraged at the beginning, while the more sensitive issues covered by parts III, IV and V might be incorporated later.

Ensuring the availability of defence White Papers is another important first step towards establishing a common approach to White Papers. If publication in large quantities is too costly for some countries, selling some copies may be one solution. Another alternative would be to use the Internet, posting the document on government web sites.

If states in the region can agree to make their White Papers comprehensive and widely available, they can then be encouraged to reach consensus on the importance of balance and consistency and standardization. Lack of balance will probably be a problem for some time, but past experience suggests that improvement is possible through discussion and suggestion.

If these first stages are successfully completed, then greater precision and reliability of information can be pursued. The exchange of views, perceptions and understanding of each nation's defence policy may make it easier to extract more precise and reliable information and data since the countries involved will have built up a certain level of mutual confidence.

Defence White Papers are not a panacea for all tensions, misperceptions and suspicions among regional neighbours. They are only one elementary step towards improving transparency and confidence. The states involved ought to take an incremental approach and avoid being too ambitious or unrealistic about the value of defence White Papers. Over time, consensus on a model defence White Paper can be broadened and deepened. Encouraging countries in this direction will not only assist in strengthening consensus on the utility of defence White Papers but may also serve to harmonize differing approaches to the publication of defence White Papers. Furthermore, discussions, dialogue and consensus of this kind can in and of themselves enhance transparency and the level of mutual confidence among regional neighbours. Such a process will take time but would make a valuable contribution to improving security and transparency in the Asia–Pacific region.

8. Developing an arms register: the SIPRI experience

Siemon T. Wezeman

I. Introduction

As the analysis in this volume clearly indicates, the development of defence-related transparency mechanisms in South-East Asia must address issues, questions and complications at the theoretical, strategic and political levels. Consensus is also needed on their structure and format and on practical matters of data collection and exchange.

For nearly three decades SIPRI has addressed questions of arms register structure, format and data collection in developing and publishing the world's only open-source arms trade register. It measures and reports trends in the quantity of transfers of major conventional weapons for all suppliers and recipients in the world going back to 1950. The SIPRI register is the only comprehensive and public source which provides information as to the volume and content of arms transfers over the entire post-1950 period, and it converts the information into constant trend-indicator values to allow for measurement of transfers over time. As such, it has proven to be invaluable in lending greater transparency and understanding to arms transfer activities at the national, regional and global levels. The de facto arms trade register for South-East Asia for the period 1975–96 is an example of the data and information generated by the SIPRI arms trade register (see the appendix).

The SIPRI register has helped innumerable researchers and policy makers to address issues related to arms transfers more effectively. As one example, the development of the UN Register of Conventional Arms (UNROCA) relied in part on the expertise and experience of the SIPRI Arms Transfers Project and its construction of and research for the SIPRI arms trade register. Similarly, as researchers and policy makers in South-East Asia and the broader Asia–Pacific region contemplate arms trade transparency mechanisms, it may be helpful to consider the approach, experience and output of the SIPRI register.

To this end, this chapter has three aims. First, it describes the structure and format of the SIPRI arms trade register and problems encountered in its construction. Second, the chapter and the appendix aim to illustrate that most of the trade in major conventional weapons is open and public knowledge. Therefore, governments should be less concerned that information provided to official transparency mechanisms is necessarily secret or sensitive. Third, information in section II below will help the reader to interpret the information contained in the appendix.

II. The SIPRI register

Selection criteria

The SIPRI arms transfer data cover six general categories of major weapons or weapon systems: (a) aircraft; (b) armoured vehicles; (c) artillery; (d) guidance and radar systems; (e) missiles; and (f) warships. The register does not include the trade in small arms, artillery under 100-mm calibre, ammunition, support items, services, components or production technology. Publicly available information is inadequate to track these items satisfactorily. There are two criteria for the selection of major weapon transfers for the register: technical parameters and military application. Table 8.1 describes the main categories and sub-categories of major conventional weapons included in the SIPRI register.[1]

The six categories are further divided into many sub-categories. The number of these is not fixed: for example, there are approximately 21 sub-categories of aircraft, such as fighters, tanker/transports, combat helicopters and trainers. If and when the need arises, a new sub-category can be developed and used. The use of sub-categories differs considerably from that of the UNROCA, where states are free to offer as much or as little detail as they want or not to submit a report at all.

Sources

The SIPRI registers are largely compiled from information contained in some 200 publications from all over the world. The sources con-

---

[1] Further information on the sources and methods used in compiling the SIPRI registers is to be found each year in the *SIPRI Yearbook* or in *Sources and Methods for SIPRI Research on Military Expenditure, Arms Transfers and Arms Production*, SIPRI Fact Sheet, Nov. 1994.

Table 8.1. Categories and sub-categories of major conventional weapons included in the annual SIPRI arms trade registers

Category	Sub-category/detail
Aircraft	Military-use aircraft including fighters, attack aircraft, trainers, military helicopters, bombers, electronic warfare, surveillance, and command and control aircraft. Transport and VIP aircraft are included if they bear military insignia or are otherwise confirmed as military-registered. Aerobatic aeroplanes and gliders are excluded; micro-light aircraft, remotely piloted vehicles and drones are also excluded although these systems are increasingly finding military applications.
Armoured vehicles	Includes all types of tank, tank destroyer, armoured car, armoured personnel carrier, armoured support vehicle and infantry combat vehicle. Military lorries, jeeps and other unarmoured support vehicles are not included.
Artillery	Includes multiple rocket launchers, self-propelled and towed guns, mortars and howitzers with a calibre equal to or above 100 mm.
Guidance and radar systems	Electronic-tracking, target-acquisition, fire-control, launch and guidance systems that are either (a) deployed independently of a weapon system listed under another weapon category (e.g., certain ground-based surface-to-air missile (SAM) launch systems) or (b) ship-borne missile-launch or point-defence close-in weapon systems (CIWS).
Missiles	Includes only guided missiles. Unguided rockets (such as man-portable anti-armour, artillery or air-launched rockets), unpowered aerial munitions (such as free-fall or laser-guided bombs), and anti-submarine rockets and torpedoes are excluded. Missiles and their guidance/launch vehicles are entered separately.
Warships	Includes all military-use ships, even if not fitted with armament, except vessels purely for research and small craft (displacement of less than 100 t) not carrying guns with a calibre equal to or above 100 mm, missiles or torpedoes.

sulted are of five general types: (a) newspapers; (b) periodicals; (c) monographs and annual reference works; (d) official publications; and (e) documents issued by international and intergovernmental organizations. These sources are all publicly available. SIPRI refrains from using confidential or classified information where the sources of

Table 8.2. Examples of sources and information: the case of the Thai light combat aircraft, 1990–95

Date	Source publication	Information given
Dec. 1990	*Armed Forces International*	RTAF interested in A-10; Tornado, Hawk and AMX also considered
5 Sep. 1991	*Interavia Air Letter*	Thai Supreme Command proposes 26 single and 12 two-seat AMXs; deal will go through after previous infighting
Sep. 1991	*Defence*	RTAF seeks approval for 36 AMX; earlier Hawk 100/200 was considered; advanced trainer still sought
8 Nov. 1991	*Flight International*	RTAF selects 38 AMX over Hawk 100/200, Tornado and F/A-18; contract could be signed in a month
22 Feb. 1992	*Jane's Defence Weekly*	Hawk 200 and AMX are competing for order of up to 38
5 Mar. 1992	*Defence News*	Parliament has authorized purchase of 36 L-39s
Apr. 1992	*Jane's Defence Weekly*	Thai Cabinet has approved request for 36 L-39ZEs; order still to be finalized; original RTAF hope was for 50 aircraft
Apr. 1992	*Military Technology*	There is a strong possibility of a sale of L-39s to Thailand
2 Apr. 1992	*Interavia Air Letter*	36 L-39s ordered
5 Apr. 1992	*Air & Cosmos*	Thailand has ordered 36 L-39s
11 Apr. 1992	*Jane's Defence Weekly*	36 L-39ZEs ordered
May 1992	*Panorama Difensa*	26 L-36ZEs ordered
21 May 1992	*Far East Economic Review*	Expected purchase of L-39s
June 1992	*Interavia Aerospace Review*	Order for 36 L-39MPs
28 June 1992	*Defense News*	Thailand bought 36 L-39ZA/MPs
July 1992	*Asia–Pacific Defence Reporter*	Cabinet approved RTAF L-39 request
Sep. 1992	*Military Technology*	RTAF and Aero have signed final contract for 36 L-39Ms (also referred to as L-59)
Mar. 1993	*Interavia/Aerospace World*	Deliveries of L-59E scheduled to start second half of 1993
5 Mar. 1994	*Jane's Defence Weekly*	Four Thai L-39s in production at Aero
Apr. 1995	*Asia Defence Journal*	Delivery of 36 L-39ZA/MPs

Note: RTAF = Royal Thai Armed Forces.

the information cannot be revealed. All data used can be tracked to a source available to any member of the public.

Because published sources often provide incomplete or conflicting information, exercising judgement and making estimates are important elements in compiling the SIPRI arms transfers database. Order and delivery dates for arms transactions are continuously revised in the light of new information, but when dates are not disclosed they are estimated by SIPRI. Where the equipment type is known but the exact number of weapons ordered and delivered is not, these are also estimated. This is most commonly done for missiles. Reports of deals involving large platforms—ships, aircraft and armoured vehicles—often ignore missile armaments. Unless there is explicit evidence that platforms were disarmed or altered before delivery, it is assumed that the platforms carry a weapons fit specified in one of the major reference works such as the *Jane's* or *Interavia* series.

Where possible SIPRI uses primary sources such as defence White Papers, official announcements by government or industry, or government reports. However, in many cases SIPRI has to rely on secondary sources. These report mostly what they learn from primary sources but do not usually identify the original sources satisfactorily. This leaves arms trade researchers uncertain as to whether their secondary sources are all quoting the same unidentified official (or unofficial) source, which may be misquoted or unreliable. It is also possible that one secondary source is quoting another secondary source without making this obvious to the researcher.

The number of sources that can be consulted is limited by staff resources and finances, access to certain regions and language skills. This means that the SIPRI register cannot be considered complete. On the other hand, it is the only globally comprehensive arms transfers register publicly available other than the UNROCA, and it provides greater detail and more information over time than the UNROCA.

To qualify for inclusion in the SIPRI register, items must be destined for the armed forces, paramilitary forces, intelligence agencies or police of another country. In considering the public record, SIPRI must decide what to include and what to ignore. Many deals and transfers reported at one point are discredited some time later. However, rumours can have a long lifetime, even despite official denials from both buyers and sellers or despite the order and delivery of some other system.[2]

In many cases the data from one source will partly overlap with data from another. In the best case the sources taken together give a complete, consistent picture of a transfer. In most cases, however, there will be a degree of inconsistency, ranging from details of the value of a transfer to contradictory statements as to whether it occurred at all. To be as accurate as possible in its reporting, SIPRI has a general rule that a transfer must be described in at least three different sources or, in cases of significant inconsistency, in at least a few consistent sources. Table 8.2 shows in detail how a certain transfer is tracked and included in the SIPRI register through reference to open-source information.

SIPRI register accuracy

Generally speaking, the SIPRI register is as good as the sources used. Transfers not reported in open sources do not appear in the SIPRI register. In the case of weapon platforms, the rule tends to be that the bigger the system, the easier it is to get reliable information on its transfer. In many cases numbers, delivery years and suppliers are not found in public sources. In other cases such information is determined years after the transfer has taken place.

Maritime systems are most easily tracked through public sources. Ships are very well covered, partly because they are not easy to hide and because they often operate outside territorial waters or are used to patrol and assist foreign merchant ships. Ships also tend to be easily counted since they use identification numbers that are often clearly displayed on their hulls, usually together with the vessel's name.

Land-oriented systems tend to be more difficult to trace. For example, in a comparison of the information for 1992 presented in the *SIPRI Yearbook 1993* with the UNROCA, the number of armoured vehicles and artillery pieces (land-based systems) reported by SIPRI

---

[2] An example for ASEAN is the 'already commissioned Exocet-equipped fast attack craft from Spanish shipbuilder Bazan' in the Philippine Navy and the order for 38 AMX ground-attack aircraft for Thailand mentioned in one source. The ships were never delivered and a tentative order was never implemented, while the AMX disappeared from the Thai shopping list after the decision was taken to purchase the L-39 and more F-16s. Examples such as this abound. da Cunha, D., 'Conventional arms and security in Southeast Asia: China and the ASEAN', eds M. Chalmers, O. Greene and Xie Zhiqiong, *Asia Pacific Security and the UN* (Department of Peace Studies, University of Bradford: Bradford, 1995), pp. 62, 64.

was one-third the number of systems provided to the UNROCA.[3] Open sources cover other land systems, such as tanks and armoured vehicles, fairly well but sometimes miss minor or logistics-related armoured vehicles, such as armoured recovery vehicles. Self-propelled artillery systems are about as well covered as armoured vehicles. Transfers in towed artillery systems are more difficult to track, particularly systems with calibres below 152 mm.

Aircraft are also very well covered by SIPRI. This may be partly because aeroplanes still enjoy a certain 'glamour' status and tend to be highly sophisticated and costly platforms. As a result a large number of journals report on aircraft. While many of these journals cater mainly to aircraft enthusiasts, they contain an enormous amount of detailed information.

Missiles are not as well covered. Only a few publications devote space to missiles, and in many cases there is no reference to the numbers of missiles ordered or delivered. It is in this category that SIPRI has to make the most of its estimates. Much of SIPRI's data on missiles may therefore be inaccurate, particularly regarding the quantities transferred, which tend to be underestimated, and the delivery schedules.

As radar and guidance systems increased in military importance, they were included in the SIPRI database in the mid-1980s. For naval systems, coverage is about as good as for ships, and recording the numbers ordered and delivered is relatively easy. For land-based systems, information on the numbers and delivery years is generally less accurate.

Few will be surprised to learn that some countries, mostly in Western Europe and North America, are well covered in the open sources, not only because both industry and government are open about their trade but also because most of the publications covering defence issues are based in these regions. On the other hand, information on Africa is extremely difficult to come by. The Soviet Union was always an information problem and today Russia and the other successor states of the Soviet Union still present difficulties to arms transfers researchers. In Asia, China, Myanmar, North Korea and Viet Nam pose the biggest problems for tracking the arms trade.

---

[3] Laurance, E. J., Wezeman, S. T. and Wulf, H., *Arms Watch: SIPRI Report on the First Year of the UN Register of Conventional Arms*, SIPRI Research Report no. 6 (Oxford University Press: Oxford, 1993), p. 79.

National production

The SIPRI register does not include procurement through national production; nor do the US Arms Control and Disarmament Agency (ACDA), the US Library of Congress Congressional Research Service (CRS) or the UNROCA. In ASEAN national production is still in a relatively early stage, but capacity is growing. Most weapons procured from national production in the ASEAN countries are produced under licence and have not been developed indigenously. Information on these licences is available, partly because the acquisition, export and licensing processes involve companies and governments in both the original designing country and the country licensing the technology. The number of possible sources for information is therefore larger, especially because the original designers are typically in countries with a high degree of transparency.

Only a few major conventional weapons are developed or co-developed in an ASEAN country: artillery, fast attack craft, some minor warships in Singapore, and the CN-235 and CN-250 transport aircraft in Indonesia. However, even for these systems, considerable open-source information is available.

Taking into account that the development of a major weapon like a combat aircraft, helicopter, missile system or armoured vehicle is becoming more and more costly, to the point where even major powers such as Germany and the UK cannot support such efforts except in collaboration, it seems that the ASEAN countries will have increasing difficulty in developing weapon systems of such importance in the future.

Public sources offer some information on national production, although not as much as on transnational transfers. Generally speaking, however, public information on national production, particularly in areas outside North America, Japan and Western Europe, is under-reported. Encouraging governments to report such information as part of their annual register submission to the UN would help close this gap in the public record.

Appendix. A de facto arms trade register for South-East Asia, 1975–96

Siemon T. Wezeman and the SIPRI Arms Transfers Project

This appendix contains a register of transfers of major conventional weapons (see chapter 8 for a complete discussion of the methodology) for the seven member countries of the Association of South-East Asian Nations (ASEAN)—Brunei, Indonesia, Malaysia, the Philippines, Singapore, Thailand and Viet Nam—and for the three most likely candidates for future membership—Cambodia, Laos and Myanmar.

The register includes both new and second-hand weapons, bought, borrowed, leased or licence-produced by or in those countries during the period 1975–96. It is organized by recipient country and year of first delivery (unlike SIPRI arms trade registers published elsewhere).

The period 1975–96 is chosen because it can be considered the 'modern' period in the history of South-East Asia.[1]

Entries in italics indicate weapons or systems that are carried by another weapon (platform). Normally these non-independent weapons or systems are delivered with the carrying platform. In the case of missiles, the figures for numbers delivered are mostly estimates based on the number and carrying capabilities of the platforms.

In the last column, the comment 'status uncertain' indicates cases in which the various sources for any of the data differ to such an extent that the data are impossible to verify or cases in which even the existence of the transfer may be doubtful.

The registers are taken from the SIPRI Arms Transfers Project database and are based on carefully screened and analysed data collected from several hundred sources (see chapter 8).

Acronyms, abbreviations and conventions used are explained at the end of the appendix.

---

[1] For a more complete argument about the 'modern' period 1975–96 and a more complete description of the problems connected with collecting and interpreting data in the South-East Asian context, see Wezeman, S. T., *East Asian Maritime Arms Acquisitions: A Database of East Asian Naval Arms Imports and Production 1975–1996* (MIMA: Kuala Lumpur, forthcoming 1997).

Brunei

Recipient/ supplier (S) or licenser (L)	No. ordered	Weapon designation	Weapon description	Year of order/ licence	Year(s) of deliveries	No. delivered/ produced	Comments
S: UK	10	AT-104	APC	(1971)	1975–76	(10)	
S: UK	1	Samson	ARV	(1976)	1978	(1)	
S: UK	16	Scorpion	Light tank	1976	1978	16	
S: Singapore	3	Waspada Class	FAC(M)	1976	1978–79	3	
S: France	(12)	MM-38 Exocet	ShShM	1976	1978–79	(12)	*For 3 Waspada Class FAC(M)s*
S: UK	2	Sultan	APC/CP	(1976)	1981	(2)	
S: FRG	6	Bo-105C	Helicopter	1979	1981	6	
S: FRG	1	Bo-105CBS	Helicopter	(1979)	1981	1	For VIP transport
S: USA	1	S-76 Spirit	Helicopter	1980	1981	1	For VIP transport
S: USA	3	Bell-212	Helicopter	1981	1982	3	
S: Italy	2	SF-260W Warrior	Trainer aircraft	(1981)	1982	2	
S: USA	7	Bell-212	Helicopter	1982	1983	(7)	
S: USA	1	S-76C	Helicopter	(1983)	1983	1	For VIP transport
S: UK	4	Blindfire	Fire control radar	1979	1983–84	(4)	Deal worth $82 m. incl. 12 Rapier SAM systems and missiles
S: UK	12	Rapier SAMS	SAM system	1979	1983–84	(12)	Deal worth $82 m. incl. missiles and 4 Blindfire radars
S: UK	(156)	*Rapier*	*SAM*	*1979*	*1983–84*	(156)	*Deal worth $82 m. incl. 12 Rapier SAM systems and 4 Blindfire radars*
S: UK	(12)	L-118 105-mm	Towed gun	1982	1984	(12)	
S: USA	1	Bell-214ST	Helicopter	(1985)	1985	1	For VIP transport
S: USA	2	S-70C	Helicopter	1986	1986	2	For VIP transport
S: Italy	4	SF-260TP	Trainer aircraft	(1989)	1990	4	
S: France	26	VAB 4x4	APC	1988	1990–91	(26)	

S:								
			Blackhawk	helicopter	(...)	1991	(1)	For VIP transport
S:	Indonesia	1	CN-235	Transport aircraft	1995	...	...	
S:	Indonesia	3	CN-235MPA	MP aircraft	1995	...	...	
S:	UK	3	Yarrow 95-m Type	Frigate	1995	...	...	Deal worth $948 m.
S:	UK	6	Hawk-100	FGA/trainer aircraft	1996	...	...	
S:	UK	4	Hawk-200	FGA aircraft	1996	...	...	
S:	USA	4	S-70A/UH-60L	Helicopter	1996	...	...	

Cambodia

S:								
S:	China	(100)	Type-60	Light tank	(1977)	1978	100	Aid; status uncertain
S:	China	(16)	F-6	Fighter aircraft	(1978)	1978	(16)	Probably ex-Chinese Air Force; aid
S:	China	(200)	Hongjian-73	Anti-tank missile	(1978)	1978	(200)	Designation uncertain
S:	China	3	MiG-17F Fresco-C	Fighter aircraft	(1978)	1978	3	Ex-Chinese Air Force; possibly trainer version
S:	USSR	2	Mi-8 Hip-C	Helicopter	1980	1980	2	
S:	USSR	(10)	PT-76	Light tank	(1983)	1983	(10)	Status uncertain
S:	USSR	(10)	T-54	Main battle tank	(1983)	1983	(10)	Status uncertain
S:	USSR	(6)	Mi-8 Hip-E	Helicopter	(1983)	1984	(6)	
S:	USSR	2	Turya Class	Patrol craft	(1984)	1984–85	2	
S:	USSR	1	Stenka Class	Patrol craft	(1984)	1985	1	
S:	USSR	(3)	Mi-24 Hind-D	Combat helicopter	(1985)	1985	(3)	
S:	Bulgaria	(16)	MiG-21bis Fishbed-N	Fighter aircraft	(1986)	1986	(16)	Ex-Bulgarian Air Force
S:	Bulgaria	(1)	MiG-21US Mongol-B	Fighter/trainer aircraft	(1986)	1986	(1)	Ex-Bulgarian Air Force
S:	USSR	2	Stenka Class	Patrol craft	(1987)	1987	2	
S:	China	6	Type-60 122-mm	Towed gun	(1986)	1988	(6)	For Khmer Rouge
S:	China	(20)	HN-5A	Portable SAM	(1988)	1988	(20)	For Khmer Rouge
S:	USSR	5	Mi-17 Hip-H	Helicopter	1988	1989	(5)	

Recipient/ supplier (S) or licenser (L)	No. ordered	Weapon designation	Weapon description	Year of order/ licence	Year(s) of deliveries	No. delivered/ produced	Comments
S: Viet Nam	100	T-55	Main battle tank	1988	1989	100	Ex-Vietnamese Army
S: USSR	(10)	BM-14-17 140-mm	MRL	(1989)	1989	(10)	Ex-Soviet Army
S: USSR	(10)	BM-21 122-mm	MRL	1989	1989	(10)	Ex-Soviet Army
S: USSR	(15)	M-46 130-mm	Towed gun	(1989)	1989	(15)	Ex-Soviet Army
S: USSR	(15)	M-1955 100-mm	Towed gun	1989	1989	(15)	Ex-Soviet Army
S: USSR	(40)	BTR-60P	APC	(1989)	1990	(40)	Ex-Soviet Army
S: USSR	5	Mi-17 Hip-H	Helicopter	1990	1990	5	
S: USSR	15	T-55	Main battle tank	1990	1990	15	Ex-Soviet Army
S: China	24	Type-59	Main battle tank	1990	1990	24	For Khmer Rouge
S: Oman	2	BN-2A Defender	Light transport plane	(1994)	1994	2	Ex-Omani Air Force
S: Ukraine	(4)	Mi-17 Hip-H	Helicopter	(1994)	1994	(4)	Second-hand; may incl. 2 Mi-8 helicopters
S: Czech Rep.	(26)	OT-64A SKOT	APC	1994	1994	26	Ex-Czech Army
S: Italy	6	P-92 Echo	Light aircraft	(1994)	1994	6	
S: Czech Rep.	40	T-55	Main battle tank	1994	1994	40	Ex-Czech Army
S: Poland	(50)	T-55	Main battle tank	1994	1994	50	Ex-Polish Army
S: Czech Rep.	6	L-39Z Albatros	Jet trainer aircraft	(1994)	1996	6	Ex-Czech Air Force; deal worth $3.6 m. incl. refurbishment and training in Israel
Indonesia							
S: Netherlands	8	F-27-500 Friendship	Transport aircraft	(1974)	1975	8	
S: USA	(20)	M-102 105-mm	Towed gun	(1971)	1975–76	(20)	Status uncertain
S: Australia	6	N-22B Missionmaster	Transport aircraft	1973	1975–76	6	For navy; aid
S: USA	3	Bell-47G	Helicopter	1975	1976	3	Ex-US Army

			JetRanger-3		(1975)	1976		
S:	USA	(2)	C-130B Hercules	Transport aircraft	1975	1976	(2)	Ex-US Air Force; MAP aid
S:	Netherlands	8	F-27-400M Friendship	Transport aircraft	1975	1976–77	8	
S:	USA	21	Musketeer Sport	Trainer aircraft	1975	1976–77	(21)	Deal worth $19 m.
S:	USA	16	OV-10F Bronco	CAS/COIN aircraft	1976	1976–87	16	
L:	FRG	(50)	Bo-105	Helicopter	(1975)	1977	(50)	
S:	USA	2	HU-16B Albatross	MP/transport aircraft	1975	1977	2	Ex-US Air Force
S:	USA	2	King Air-100	Light transport plane	(1976)	1977–78	2	
S:	Netherlands	(100)	AMX-VCI	APC	1977	1978	(100)	Ex-Dutch Army; refurbished before delivery
S:	France	6	SA-330L Puma	Helicopter	(1978)	1978	6	
S:	Australia	8	Bell-47G-3	Helicopter	1978	1978	8	Ex-Australian Army
S:	USA	16	Bell-205/UH-1H	Helicopter	1978	1978	16	For army
S:	USA	1	C-130/L-100-30	Transport aircraft	1978	1978	1	For VIP transport
S:	USA	16	T-34C-1 Turbo Mentor	Trainer aircraft	1978	1978	16	Deal worth $8.4 m.
S:	Netherlands	(130)	AMX-13/105	Light tank	(1978)	1978–79	(130)	Ex-Dutch Army; refurbished before delivery
S:	USA	60	Commando V-150	APC	(1977)	1978–79	(60)	
L:	Spain	(30)	CN-212-100 Aviocar	Transport aircraft	1976	1978–92	(30)	More produced for export and civil customers
S:	Australia	6	N-22B Missionmaster	Transport aircraft	1977	1979	6	For navy; aid
S:	Netherlands	3	*Fatahillah Class*	*Frigate*	1975	1979–80	3	
S:	*France*	(24)	*MM-38 Exocet*	*ShShM*	*1975*	1979–80	(24)	*For 3 Fatahillah Class frigates*
S:	*Sweden*	3	*TAK-120 L46*	*Naval gun*	(1975)	1979–80	3	*For 3 Fatahillah Class frigates*
S:	South Korea	4	*PSMM-5 Type*	*FAC(M)*	1976	1979–80	4	Indonesian designation Mandau Class
S:	*France*	(32)	*MM-38 Exocet*	*ShShM*	*1976*	1979–80	(32)	*For 4 PSMM-5 Type (Mandau Class) FAC(M)s*
S:	USA	3	C-130H Hercules	Transport aircraft	1979	1979–81	3	

Recipient/ supplier (S) or licenser (L)	No. ordered	Weapon designation	Weapon description	Year of order/ licence	Year(s) of deliveries	No. delivered/ produced	Comments
S: France	14	TRS-2230/15	Surveillance radar	1978	1979–81	(14)	
S: Israel	16	A-4E Skyhawk	FGA aircraft	1979	1980	16	Ex-Israeli Air Force; delivered via USA; deal worth $25.8 m.; incl. 2 TA-4H FGA/trainer aircraft
S: USA	16	F-5E Tiger-2	FGA aircraft	1977	1980	16	Deal worth $108 m.; incl. 4 F-5F FGA/trainer aircraft
S: USA	(96)	AIM-9J Sidewinder	Air-to-air missile	1977	1980	(96)	For 16 F-5E/F FGA aircraft
S: UK	8	Hawk Mk-53	Jet trainer aircraft	1978	1980–81	(8)	Deal worth $45.5 m.
S: USA	5	C-130H-30 Hercules	Transport aircraft	1979	1980–81	5	
S: FRG	2	Type-209/1300	Submarine	1977	1981	2	Indonesian designation Cakra Class
S: Yugoslavia	1	Dewantara Class	Training ship/frigate	1978	1981	1	
S: France	(12)	MM-38 Exocet	ShShM	(1978)	1981	(12)	For 1 Dewantara Class training ship/ frigate
S: South Korea	4	Alligator Class	Landing ship	1979	1981	4	Indonesian designation Teluk Semangka Class
S: Switzerland	20	AS-202 Bravo	Trainer aircraft	1980	1981	20	Deal worth $3.5 m.
S: USA	(5)	T-41A Mescalero	Trainer aircraft	(1980)	1981	(5)	
S: UK	4	Hawk Mk-53	Jet trainer aircraft	1981	1981	4	Deal worth $37 m.
S: Australia	6	N-22L Searchmaster	MP aircraft	1980	1981–82	6	For navy; aid
L: France	(7)	SA-330L Puma	Helicopter	1980	1981–83	(7)	
S: Netherlands	10	Wasp HAS-1	ASW helicopter	1981	1981–82	10	Ex-Dutch Navy; for navy
S: France	3	C-160F Transall	Transport aircraft	1979	1982	3	
S: USA	1	Jetfoil Type	Patrol craft	1980	1982	1	For evaluation; Indonesian designation Bima Samudera Class

Supplier	No. ordered	Weapon designation	Weapon description	Year of order	Year of delivery	No. delivered	Comments
S: France	(40)	AMX-10P	AIFV	1981	1982	(20)	
S: USA	1	Boeing-737-200C	Transport aircraft	1981	1982	1	For VIP transport
S: USA	2	C-130H-30 Hercules	Transport aircraft	1981	1982	2	
S: USA	1	C-130H-MP Hercules	MP/transport aircraft	1981	1982	1	
S: Sweden	(5)	Giraffe-40	Surveillance radar	(1981)	1982	(5)	
S: USA	133	M-101A1 105-mm	Towed gun	(1981)	1982	(133)	Ex-US Army
S: Sweden	(150)	RBS-70	Portable SAM	(1981)	1982	(150)	
S: Australia	3	Attack Class	Patrol craft	(1981)	1982–83	3	Ex-Australian Navy; refitted before delivery; Indonesian designation Sibarau Class
S: USA	2	Boeing-737 Surveiller	MP aircraft	1981	1983	2	
S: UK	5	Hawk Mk-53	Jet trainer aircraft	1982	1983	5	
S: USA	6	Bell-212	Helicopter	1982	1983	6	
S: USA	9	Hughes-300C	Helicopter	1982	1983	9	For training
S: USA	6	Bell-412	Helicopter	1983	1983	6	Prior to licensed production
S: USA	22	Commando Ranger APC	APC	(1983)	1983	22	Deal worth $9.6 m. incl. 28 Commando Scout scout cars
S: USA	28	Commando Scout	Scout car	1983	1983	28	Deal worth $9.6 m. incl. 22 Commando Ranger APCs
S: USA	(6)	PA-38 Tomahawk	Trainer aircraft	(1983)	1983	(6)	Delivered via Singapore
S: USA	16	A-4E Skyhawk	FGA aircraft	1981	1984	16	Ex-US Navy; deal worth $27 m.
S: FRG	2	PB-57 Type	Patrol craft	1982	1984	2	Prior to licensed production
S: UK	3	Hawk Mk-53	Jet trainer aircraft	1983	1984	3	
S: USA	9	T-34C-1 Turbo Mentor	Trainer aircraft	1983	1984	9	Deal worth $12.4 m.

Recipient/ supplier (S) or licenser (L)	No. ordered	Weapon designation	Weapon description	Year of order/ licence	Year(s) of deliveries	No. delivered/ produced	Comments
S: USA	4	Jetfoil Type	Patrol craft	1983	1984–86	4	Option on 6 more not used and planned licensed production of 36 abandoned; Indo-Ex-Australian Navy; refitted before deliv-ery;
S: Australia	3	Attack Class	Patrol craft	(1984)	1985–86	3	Indonesian designation Sibarau Class
S: UK	3	Tribal Class	Frigate	1984	1985–86	3	Ex-British Navy; refitted before delivery; Indonesian designation Tiyahahu Class
S: UK	(48)	*Seacat*	*ShAM*	*1984*	*1985–86*	*(48)*	*For 3 Tribal Class frigates*
S: UK	(20)	Rapier SAMS	SAM system	1985	1985–86	(20)	Deal worth $100 m. incl. missiles
S: UK	(240)	*Improved Rapier*	*SAM*	*1985*	*1985–86*	*(120)*	*Deal worth $100 m. incl. 20 Rapier SAM systems*
L: France	(9)	AS-332B Super Puma	Helicopter	1983	1985–93	9	More produced for export and civil customers
S: UK	1	Hecla Class	Survey ship	1985	1986	1	Ex-British Navy; Indonesian designation Dewa Kember Class
S: Netherlands	(50)	AMX Mk-61 105-mm	Self-propelled gun	(1984)	1986–87	(50)	Ex-Dutch Army
L: FRG	(4)	BK-117	Helicopter	1982	1986–88	4	More produced for civil customers
S: UK	(25)	Rapier SAMS	SAM system	1984	1986–88	(25)	Deal worth $128 m. incl. missiles
S: UK	(300)	*Improved Rapier*	*SAM*	*1984*	*1986–88*	*(300)*	*Deal worth $128 m. incl. 25 Rapier SAM systems*
S: Netherlands	4	Van Speijk Class	Frigate	1986	1986–88	4	Ex-Dutch Navy; deal worth $120 m.; Indonesian designation Ahmed Yani Class
S: USA	(64)	*RGM-84A Harpoon*	*ShShM*	*(1986)*	*1986–88*	*(64)*	*For 4 Van Speijk Class frigates; status uncertain*
S: Netherlands	(64)	*Seacat*	*ShAM*	*1986*	*1986–88*	*(64)*	*For 4 Van Speijk Class frigates*

for civil customers

	Country	No.	Weapon designation	Description	Year of order	Year(s) of delivery	No. delivered	Comments
S:	UK	(10)	Rapier SAMS	SAM system	1986	1987	(10)	Deal worth $60 m. incl. missiles
S:	UK	(120)	*Improved Rapier*	*SAM*	*1986*	*1987*	*(120)*	*Deal worth $60 m. incl. 10 Rapier SAM systems*
S:	Netherlands	2	Alkmaar Class	MCM ship	1985	1988	2	Indonesian designation Palau Rengat Class
L:	FRG	6	PB-57 Type	Patrol craft	1982	1988–92	6	
L:	FRG	(48)	Bo-105	Helicopter	1987	1988–93	(48)	Incl. production for civil customers
S:	Netherlands	2	Van Speijk Class	Frigate	1989	1989	2	Ex-Dutch Navy; Indonesian designation Ahmed Yani Class
S:	USA	(32)	RGM-84A	ShShM	(1989)	1989	(64)	*For 2 Van Speijk Class frigates; status uncertain.*
S:	*Netherlands*	(32)	Seacat	ShAM	1989	1989	(64)	*For 2 Van Speijk Class frigates*
S:	USA	12	F-16A Fighting	FGA aircraft	1986	1989–90	(12)	'Peace Bima-Sena' programme worth $337 m. (offsets $52 m.); incl. 4 F-16B FGA/trainer aircraft
S:	USA	(72)	*AIM-9P Sidewinder*	*Air-to-air missile*	*(1986)*	*1989–90*	*(72)*	*For 12 F-16A/B FGA aircraft*
S:	UK	(14)	AR-325	Surveillance radar	1989	1991–95	(10)	
S:	UK	1	Rover Class	Oiler	1991	1992	1	Ex-British Navy; refitted before delivery
S:	FRG	12	Frosch-1 Class	Landing ship	1992	1993–95	(12)	Former GDR ships; refitted before delivery
S:	FRG	16	Parchim Class	Corvette	1992	1993–96	(16)	Former GDR ships; refitted before delivery
S:	FRG	9	Kondor Class	Minesweeper	1992	1994	9	Former GDR ships; refitted before delivery
S:	UAE	4	DHC-5 Buffalo	Transport aircraft	(1995)	1995	4	Ex-UAE Air Force
S:	FRG	2	Frosch-2 Class	Supply ship	1992	1995	2	Former GDR ships; refitted before delivery
S:	France	20	LG-1 105-mm	Towed gun	1994	1995–96	(20)	Deal worth $15 m. incl. ammunition; for marines
S:	UK	(30)	Scorpion-90	Light tank	1995	1995–96	(30)	
S:	UK	(20)	Stormer	APC	1995	1995–96	(20)	Incl. 2 APC/CP and several vehicles in an ambulance version

Recipient/ supplier (S) or licenser (L)	No. ordered	Weapon designation	Weapon description	Year of order/ licence	Year(s) of deliveries	No. delivered/ produced	Comments
S: UK	14	Hawk-100	FGA/trainer aircraft	1993	1996	(8)	Option on 16 more
S: UK	10	Hawk-200	FGA aircraft	1993	:	:	
L: FRG	4	PB-57 Type	Patrol craft	1993	:	:	Indonesian designation Singa Class
S: FRG	5	Wiesel	Scout car	1996	:	:	
S: FRG	2	Wiesel-2	APC	1996	:	:	
Philippines							
S: Singapore	2	Bataan Class	Patrol craft	(1973)	1975	2	
S: UK	5	BN-2A Defender	Light transport plane	(1974)	1975	5	For navy; for SAR and maritime patrol
S: USA	1	C-130/L-100-20	Transport aircraft	(1974)	1975	1	
S: USA	1	Admirable Class	Minesweeper	1975	1975	1	Ex-South Vietnamese Navy; returned to USA and given to Philippines
S: USA	1	PC-452 Type	Patrol craft	(1975)	1975	1	Ex-Cambodian Navy; returned to USA and given to Philippines
S: USA	4	LSIL Type	Landing craft	(1975)	1975	4	Ex-South Vietnamese Navy; returned to USA and given to Philippines
S: USA	1	LST-511 Class	Landing ship	1975	1975	1	Ex-South Vietnamese Navy; returned to USA and given to Philippines
S: USA	1	T-610 Super Pinto	CAS/COIN aircraft	(1975)	1975	1	Prior to planned licensed production
S: Australia	12	N-22B Missionmaster	Transport aircraft	(1974)	1975–76	(12)	
S: USA	3	PCE-827 Class	Corvette	1975	1975–76	3	Ex-South Vietnamese Navy; returned to USA and given to Philippines
L: UK	20	BN-2A Islander	Light transport plane	1974	1975–89	(20)	55 more built for civil customers
S: USA	6	Barnegat Class	Depot ship	1975	1976	6	Ex-South Vietnamese Navy; returned to USA and given to Philippines

Supplier	No. ordered	Weapon designation	Weapon description	Year of order	Year of delivery	No. delivered	Comments
							and given to Philippines
S: USA	3	LSM Type	Landing craft	1975	1976	3	Ex-South Vietnamese Navy; returned to USA and given to Philippines
S: USA	3	LSSL Type	Gunboat	1975	1976	3	Ex-South Vietnamese Navy; returned to USA and given to Philippines
S: USA	4	LST-1 Class	Landing ship	1976	1976	4	Ex-US Navy; refitted in Japan before delivery
S: USA	6	LST-511 Class	Landing ship	1976	1976	6	Ex-US Navy; refitted in Japan before delivery
S: USA	1	PGM-71 Class	Patrol craft	1975	1976	1	Ex-South Vietnamese Navy; returned to USA and given to Philippines
S: USA	20	M-113A1	APC	1976	1976	20	
S: USA	(4)	HU-16B Albatross	MP/transport aircraft	1975	1976–77	(4)	Ex-US Navy
S: USA	6	C-130H Hercules	Transport aircraft	1976	1976–78	5	
L: FRG	(13)	Bo-105C	Helicopter	1974	1976–89	(13)	More produced for civil customers
S: South Vietnam	2	LST-511 Class	Landing ship	1975	1977	2	Ex-South Vietnamese Navy; escaped to Philippines in 1975 and bought 1977
S: USA	17	Bell-205/UH-1H	Helicopter	1976	1977	17	
S: USA	(3)	RT-33A T-Bird	Recce aircraft	(1976)	1977	(3)	Ex-US Air Force
S: UK	(41)	Scorpion	Light tank	1976	1977	(41)	
S: USA	1	Achelous Class	Repair ship	1977	1977	1	Ex-US Navy
S: USA	3	Cannon Class	Frigate	(1975)	1978	3	Ex-Japanese Navy; returned to USA and given to Philippines; refitted in South Korea before delivery
S: USA	35	F-8H Crusader	Fighter aircraft	1977	1978	35	Ex-US Navy; deal worth $34.7 m. incl. 25 refurbished before delivery and 10 for spares only
S: USA	(25)	M-113A1	APC	(1977)	1978	(25)	
S: USA	(100)	LVTP-5	APC	(1978)	1978–79	(100)	Ex-US Marines; for marines
S: USA	45	AIFV-APC	APC	1975	1979	45	
S: Japan	3	LCU-1466 Class	Landing craft	1975	1979	3	Ex-Japanese Navy; refitted before delivery

Recipient/ supplier (S) or licenser (L)	No. ordered	Weapon designation	Weapon description	Year of order/ licence	Year(s) of deliveries	No. delivered/ produced	Comments
S: Australia	4	Kagitingan Class	Patrol craft	(1977)	1979	4	Prior to planned licensed production
S: Japan	3	LST-511 Class	Landing ship	1978	1979	3	Ex-Japanese Navy; refitted before delivery
S: Portugal	(20)	Chaimite	APC	(1978)	1979–80	(20)	
S: USA	(20)	T-28D Trojan	Trainer aircraft	(1978)	1979–81	(20)	Ex-US Navy
S: USA	6	AIFV-ARV	ARV	1979	1980	(6)	
S: USA	18	Bell-205/UH-1H	Helicopter	1980	1980	(18)	Deal worth $21.6 m.
S: USA	20	M-113A1	APC	(1980)	1981	(20)	
S: Netherlands	3	F-27 Maritime	MP aircraft	1980	1981–82	3	Deal worth $8.5 m.; option on 2 more not used
S: USA	(97)	M-102 105-mm	Towed gun	(1978)	1981–84	(97)	
S: USA	3	Centurion	Light aircraft	(1981)	1982	(3)	
S: USA	10	Commando V-150	APC	1982	1982	10	
S: Italy	(120)	Model-56	Towed gun	(1982)	1982–85	(120)	Number and delivery schedule uncertain
S: USA	15	Bell-205/UH-1H	Helicopter	1982	1983	15	Ex-US Army; deal worth $36 m.; refurbished before delivery
S: USA	12	Bell-205/UH-1H	Helicopter	1983	1983	12	Ex-US Army; deal worth $22 m.; refurbished before delivery
S: USA	2	Bell-212	Helicopter	(1983)	1984	2	For VIP transport
S: USA	2	Bell-214A	Helicopter	(1983)	1984	2	For VIP transport
S: USA	17	S-76 Spirit	Helicopter	1983	1983	17	Deal worth $60 m. incl. 2 S-70/UH-60 helicopters; incl. 12 armed version, 2 for SAR and 3 for VIP transport
S: USA	2	S-70/UH-60 Blackhawk	Helicopter	1983	1984	2	Deal worth $60 m. incl. 17 S-76 helicopters
S: USA	100	Commando V-150	APC	1983	1984–85	(100)	
S: USA	55	LVTP-7A1	APC	1982	1984–85	(55)	Deal worth $64 m.; for marines
S: USA	4	Series-320	Surveillance radar	(1984)	1984–85	(4)	

	Country	No.	Designation	Type	Order	Delivery	Del.	Comments
S:	Indonesia	2	C-212-200	Transport aircraft	(1986)	1986	2	Ex-Indonesian Air Force; 3-month loan
S:	USA	2	S-70C	Helicopter	(1985)	1986	(2)	Status uncertain
S:	USA	10	Bell-205/UH-1H	Helicopter	1987	1987	10	
S:	USA	25	Commando V-150S	APC	1987	1988	25	Deal worth $6.9 m.
S:	USA	7	T-33A T-Bird	Jet trainer aircraft	1987	1988	7	Ex-US Air Force; deal worth $1.4 m.; aid
S:	USA	4	F-5A Freedom Fighter	FGA aircraft	1988	1989	4	Ex-Taiwanese Air Force
L:	FRG	(4)	Bo-105C	Helicopter	(1988)	1989–92	(4)	For navy
S:	Italy	24	S-211	Jet trainer aircraft	1988	1989–94	24	Assembled from kits; option on 12 more
S:	Australia	4	N-24A Nomad	Transport aircraft	1989	1990	4	Deal worth $5.3 m.
S:	USA	10	Bell-205/UH-1H	Helicopter	(1990)	1992–93	(10)	Ex-US Army
S:	Italy	18	SF-260TP	Trainer aircraft	1992	1993–94	(18)	Deal worth $52 m.; assembled from kits
S:	UK	8	Simba	APC	1992	1993–94	8	Deal worth $46 m. incl. licensed production of 142
S:	USA	22	Hughes-500D	Helicopter	1988	1990–92	22	Deal worth $25 m.; aid
S:	USA	24	OV-10F Bronco	CAS/COIN aircraft	1991	1991–92	24	Ex-US Air Force
S:	USA	8	MD-530MG Defender	Helicopter	1992	1992–93	8	Deal worth $11 m.
S:	USA	3	Besson Class	Landing ship	1992	1993–94	3	
S:	USA	5	MD-530MG Defender	Helicopter	1993	1994–95	(5)	
S:	Russia	20	Yak-18T	Light aircraft	(1993)	1994–95	(10)	
L:	UK	142	FS-100 Simba	APC	1992	1994–96	(121)	Deal worth $46 m. incl. 8 delivered direct; incl. 4 assembled from kits
S:	USA	12	Commando V-300	APC	1993	1995	(12)	Deal worth $18.2 m. incl. 12 Commando V-300/FSV AIFVs
S:	USA	12	Commando V-300/FSV	AIFV	1993	1995	(12)	Deal worth $18.2 m. incl. 12 Commando V-300 APCs

Recipient/ supplier (S) or licenser (L)	No. ordered	Weapon designation	Weapon description	Year of order/ licence	Year(s) of deliveries	No. delivered/ produced	Comments
S: South Korea	3	F-5A Freedom Fighter	FGA aircraft	(1995)	1995	3	Ex-South Korean Air Force; aid
S: South Korea	5	Sea Dolphin Class	Patrol craft	1995	1995	5	Ex-South Korean Navy; aid
Laos							
S: USSR	(15)	T-54	Main battle tank	(1973)	1975	(15)	Ex-Soviet Army; status and designation uncertain; could be PT-76 light tank
S: USSR	15	T-55	Main battle tank	(1973)	1975	(15)	Ex-Soviet Army; status and designation uncertain; could be PT-76 light tank
S: USSR	(6)	An-2 Colt	Light transport plane	(1976)	1976	(6)	Possibly second-hand
SSR	6	An-24 Coke	Transport aircraft	1976	1976–77	6	
S: USSR	(6)	Mi-8 Hip-C	Helicopter	1976	1976–77	(6)	
S: USSR	12	MiG-21F Fishbed-C	Fighter aircraft	1976	1977	12	Ex-Soviet Air Force; gift; incl. 2 MiG-21U fighter/trainer aircraft
S: USSR	(60)	AA-2 Atoll	Air-to-air missile	1976	1977	(60)	For 10 MiG-21F fighter aircraft
S: USSR	2	Yak-40 Codling	Transport aircraft	1976	1977	2	For VIP transport
S: USSR	3	An-26 Curl-A	Transport aircraft	1978	1978	3	
S: USSR	4	MiG-21F Fishbed-C	Fighter aircraft	(1981)	1981	4	Ex-Soviet Air Force
S: USSR	(35)	BTR-60P	APC	(1980)	1981–82	(35)	Status and designation uncertain; could be BTR-152
S: USSR	(10)	D-30 122mm	Towed gun	(1982)	1983	(10)	Status uncertain
S: USSR	(16)	MiG-21F Fishbed-C	Fighter aircraft	(1982)	1983	(16)	Ex-Soviet Air Force
S: USSR	(3)	SA-2 SAMS	SAM system	(1983)	1984	(3)	Status uncertain
S: USSR	(27)	SA-2 Guideline	SAM	(1983)	1984	(27)	Status uncertain; for 3 SA-2 SAM systems

	No.	Weapon designation	Weapon description	Year of order	Year of delivery	No. delivered	Comments
S: *USSR*	*(18)*	*SA-3 Goa*	*SAM*	*(1983)*	*1984*	*(18)*	*Status uncertain; for 3 SA-3 SAM systems*
S: USSR	(40)	SA-7 Grail	Portable SAM	(1983)	1984	(40)	Status uncertain; ex-Soviet Army
S: USSR	(3)	ZSU-57-2	AAV(G)	(1983)	1984	(3)	Ex-Soviet Army; status uncertain
S: USSR	(10)	M-46 130mm	Towed gun	(1984)	1985	(10)	Ex-Soviet Air Force
S: USSR	(12)	MiG-21MF Fishbed-J	Fighter aircraft	(1985)	1985	(12)	Ex-Soviet Air Force
S: USSR	(26)	MiG-21F Fishbed-C	Fighter aircraft	(1987)	1987	(26)	Ex-Soviet Air Force
S: USSR	(2)	Mi-6 Hook-A	Helicopter	1987	1987–88	2	Ex-Soviet Air Force
S: Romania	144	SA-7 Grail	Portable SAM	1989	1989	144	
S: China	2	Y-12	Transport aircraft	(1990)	1990	2	
Malaysia							
S: USA	12	Cessna-402B	Light transport plane	1974	1975	12	Incl. 4 for photographic survey
S: Netherlands	2	F-28-1000 Fellowship	Transport aircraft	1974	1975	2	
S: USA	14	F-5E Tiger-2	FGA aircraft	1972	1975–76	(14)	*For 14 F-5E fighters*
S: *USA*	*(120)*	*AIM-9J Sidewinder*	*Air-to-air missile*	*(1972)*	*1975–76*	*(120)*	
S: USA	6	C-130H Hercules	Transport aircraft	1974	1976	6	Deal worth $48 m. incl. spares
S: USA	2	LST-511 Class	Landing ship	1974	1976	2	Ex-US Navy; Malaysian designation Sri Langkawi Class
L: FRG	6	FPB-45 Type	Patrol craft	1973	1976–77	6	Malaysian designation Jerong Class
S: *Netherlands*	*6*	*WM-28*	*Fire control radar*	*1973*	*1976–77*	*(6)*	*For 6 FPB-45 Type (Jerong Class) patrol craft*
S: Sweden	2	9LV-200 Mk-2	Fire control radar	(1983)	1985–87	(2)	For 2 Musytari Class OPVs
S: Sweden	4	Handalan Class	FAC(M)	1976	1979	4	Deal worth $157 m.
S: *Sweden*	*4*	*9GR-600*	*Surveillance radar*	*1976*	*1979*	*4*	*On 4 Handalan Class FAC(M)s*
S: *Sweden*	*4*	*9LV-200 Mk-2*	*Fire control radar*	*1976*	*1979*	*4*	*On 4 Handalan Class FAC(M)s*

Recipient/ supplier (S) or licenser (L)	Weapon designation	No. ordered	Weapon description	Year of order/ licence	Year(s) of deliveries	No. delivered/ produced	Comments
S: France	MM-38 Exocet	(32)	ShShM	1976	1979	(32)	For 4 Handalan Class FAC(M)s
S: UK	Mermaid Class	1	Frigate	(1976)	1977	1	Ex-British Navy; Malaysian designation Hang Tuah Class
S: USA	S-61A-4	(8)	Helicopter	1976	1977	(8)	Malaysian designation Nuri
S: Italy	Model-56 105mm	92	Towed gun	(1976)	1977–79	(92)	
S: Italy	Bell-212/AB-212	(5)	Helicopter	1974	1978	(5)	
S: USA	Bell-206B JetRanger-3	5	Helicopter	1975	1978	5	
L: FRG	Mutiara Class	1	Survey ship	1975	1978	1	
S: Singapore	SA-316B Alouette-3	7	Helicopter	1978	1978	7	Ex-Singaporean Air Force
S: UK	AT-105 Saxon	44	APC	1977	1978–79	(44)	Deal worth $4.7 m.
S: USA	S-61A-4	16	Helicopter	1977	1978–79	(16)	Malaysian designation Nuri
S: USA	Commando V-150	(130)	APC	1977	1978–79	(130)	
S: UK	Blowpipe	(128)	Portable SAM	1976	1979	(128)	For army
S: USA	C-130H-MP Hercules	3	MP/transport aircraft	1979	1980	3	Deal worth $27.5 m.
S: FRG	Sri Indera Class	1	Support ship	1979	1980	1	
S: USA	F-5F Tiger-2	5	FGA/trainer aircraft	(1980)	1981	5	Deal worth $25 m.; incl. 1 F-5E FGA aircraft
S: USA	AIM-9L Sidewinder	(30)	Air-to-air missile	(1980)	1981	(30)	For 5 F-5E/F FGA aircraft
S: USA	A-4C Skyhawk	25	FGA/trainer aircraft	1981	1981–82	(25)	Ex-US Navy; for spares only
S: USA	A-4L Skyhawk	23	FGA/trainer aircraft	1981	1981–82	(23)	Ex-US Navy; for storage in USA as source for spares or later refurbishment to A-4PTM

							Hitam Class
S:	FRG	459	Condor	APC	1981	1982–84	(459)	Incl. APC/CP, ambulance and ARV versions
S:	USA	2	RF-5E Tigereye	Recce aircraft	1980	1983	2	Deal worth $38.2 m.
S:	South Korea	1	Sri Indera Class	Support ship	1981	1983	1	Built under licence from FRG; in addition to 1 delivered from FRG
S:	UK	26	Scorpion-90	Light tank	1982	1983	26	Deal worth $40 m. incl. 25 Stormer APCs
S:	UK	(20)	Shorland SB-301	APC	(1982)	1983	(20)	For police
S:	UK	25	Stormer	APC	1982	1983	25	Deal worth $40 m. incl. 26 Scorpion-90 light tanks
S:	Switzerland	44	PC-7 Turbo Trainer	Trainer aircraft	1981	1983–84	(44)	Deal worth $53 m.; incl. some for close support role
S:	Italy	12	MB-339A	Jet trainer aircraft	1982	1983–84	(12)	Option on 14 more not used
S:	Belgium	162	Sibmas-90	AIFV	1981	1983–85	(162)	Deal worth $94 m. incl. 24 Sibmas/ARVs
S:	Canada	2	Challenger-600	Transport aircraft	(1981)	1984	2	For VIP transport
S:	FRG	2	FS-1500 Type	Frigate	1981	1984	2	Malaysian designation Kasturi Class
S:	France	2	100mm Compact	Naval gun	(1981)	1984	2	*For 2 FS-1500 Type (Kasturi Class) frigates*
S:	Netherlands	2	DA-08	Surveillance radar	1981	1984	2	*For 2 FS-1500 Type (Kasturi Class) frigates*
S:	France	(16)	MM-38 Exocet	ShShM	1981	1984	(16)	*For 2 FS-1500 Type (Kasturi Class) frigates*
S:	Netherlands	2	WM-22	Fire control radar	1981	1984	2	*For 2 FS-1500 Type (Kasturi Class) frigates*
S:	Belgium	24	Sibmas/ARV	ARV	1981	1984–85	(24)	Deal worth $94 m. incl. 165 Sibmas-90 AIFVs
S:	USA	40	A-4L Skyhawk	FGA aircraft	1981	1984–86	(40)	Ex-US Navy; refurbished to 34 A-4PTM and 6 TA-4PTM before delivery
S:	Italy	4	Lerici Class	MCM ship	1981	1985	4	Malaysian designation Mahamiru Class
S:	South Korea	1	Musytari Class	OPV	1983	1985	1	Prior to licensed production
S:	Italy	1	MB-339A	Jet trainer aircraft	(1985)	1985	1	

Recipient/ supplier (S) or licenser (L)	No. ordered	Weapon designation	Weapon description	Year of order/ licence	Year(s) of deliveries	No. delivered/ produced	Comments
S: *France*	2	*100mm Compact*	*Naval gun*	*(1983)*	*1985–87*	2	*For 2 Musytari Class OPVs*
S: *Netherlands*	2	*DA-05*	*Surveillance radar*	*1983*	*1985–87*	2	*For 2 Musytari Class OPVs*
S: USA	2	HU-16B Albatross	ASW/MP aircraft	1985	1986	2	Ex-US Navy; deal worth $8 m.; refurbished before delivery
L: South Korea	1	Musytari Class	OPV	(1983)	1986	1	
S: USA	(1)	HADR	Surveillance radar	(1982)	1986	(1)	
S: UK	6	Wasp HAS-1	ASW helicopter	1987	1988	6	Ex-British Navy; deal worth $0.85 m.; for navy
S: Indonesia	1	AS-332B Super Puma	Helicopter	1987	1988	1	For VIP transport
S: UK	9	FH-70 155-mm	Towed gun	1988	1989	9	
S: UK	6	Wasp HAS-1	ASW helicopter	1988	1989	6	Ex-British Navy; for navy
S: France	1	Mystère-Falcon 900	Transport aircraft	1988	1989	1	For VIP transport
S: Italy	4	Skyguard	Fire control radar	1988	1989	(4)	For use with 9 GDF-005 35-mm AA guns
S: Italy	4	A-109 Hirundo	Helicopter	(1988)	1990	4	For VIP transport
S: UK	(480)	Javelin	Portable SAM	1988	1991	(480)	Deal also incl. 48 launchers
S: USA	1	C-130H-MP Hercules	MP/transport aircraft	(1990)	1991	1	
S: UK	2	Martello-743D	Surveillance radar	1990	1992–95	(2)	Deal worth $190 m. incl. C³I network
S: South Korea	42	KIFV	APC	(1993)	1993	42	Deal worth $25 m.; for use with Malaysian UN forces in Bosnia
S: South Korea	21	KIFV	APC	1994	1994	(21)	Deal worth $13.2 m.; incl. 1 ARV, 1 APC/CP and 1 ambulance version
S: USA	4	B-200T Maritime	MP aircraft	1992	1994	4	

No. ordered	Supplier	Weapon designation	Weapon description	Year of order	Year of delivery	No. delivered	Comments
							aircraft
3	S: UK	FH-70 155-mm	Towed gun	1993	1994	3	
1	S: USA	Newport Class	Landing ship	1994	1994	1	Ex-US Navy; deal worth $18.3 m.; Malaysian designation Sri Indrapura Class
18	S: UK	Hawk-200	FGA aircraft	1990	1994–95	(18)	Deal worth $740 m. incl. 10 Hawk-100 FGA/trainer aircraft
504	S: UK	Starburst	Portable SAM	1993	1995–96	(252)	
47	S: South Korea	KIFV	APC	1995	1995	47	Deal worth $30 m.; incl. some APC/CP vers.
6	S: Indonesia	CN-235	Transport aircraft	1995	1995	6	Option on more; deal worth $102 m. (offsets incl. Indonesian order for 20 MD-3-160 trainer aircraft and cars)
18	S: Russia	MiG-29S Fulcrum-C	FGA aircraft	1994	1995	18	Deal worth $600 m. (offsets $220 m. incl. $150 m. barter); incl. 2 MiG-29UB FGA/trainer aircraft
(105)	*S: Russia*	*AA-10a Alamo*	*Air-to-air missile*	*1994*	*1995*	*(105)*	*For 18 MiG-29S/UB FGA aircraft*
(216)	*S: Russia*	*AA-11 Archer*	*Air-to-air missile*	*1994*	*1995*	*(216)*	*For 18 MiG-29S/UB FGA aircraft*
(96)	*S: Russia*	*AA-12 Adder*	*Air-to-air missile*	*(1994)*	*1995*	*(96)*	*For 16 MiG-29S FGA aircraft*
5	S: USA	C-130H-30 Hercules	Transport aircraft	1995	1995	5	
20	L: Switzerland	MD3-160	Trainer aircraft	1993	1995–96	(20)	More built for export and civil customers
2	S: UK	Lekiu Class	Frigate	1992		..	Deal worth $600 m. incl. spares, training and support
2	*S: Netherlands*	*DA-08*	*Surveillance radar*	*1992*		:	*For 2 Lekiu Class frigates*
16	*S: France*	*MM-40 Exocet*	*ShShM*	*1993*		:	*For 2 Lekiu Class frigates*
2	*S: Sweden*	*Sea Giraffe-150*	*Surveillance radar*	*1992*		:	*For 2 Lekiu Class frigates*
32	*S: UK*	*Seawolf VL*	*ShAM*	*1993*		:	*For 2 Lekiu Class frigates*
4	*S: UK*	*ST-1802SW*	*Fire control radar*	*1992*		:	*On 2 Lekiu Class frigates*
8	*S: USA*	*F/A-18D Hornet*	*FGA/trainer aircraft*	*1993*		:	Option on 10 more (offsets $250 m.)

Recipient/supplier (S) or licenser (L)	No. ordered	Weapon designation	Weapon description	Year of order/ licence	Year(s) of deliveries	No. delivered/ produced	Comments
S: USA	30	AGM-65D Maverick	ASM	1993	..	..	*For F/A-18D FGA aircraft*
S: USA	25	AGM-84A Harpoon	Air-to-ship missile	1993	..	..	*For F/A-18D FGA aircraft*
S: USA	20	AIM-7M Sparrow	Air-to-air missile	1993	..	..	*For F/A-18D FGA aircraft*
S: USA	40	AIM-9S Sidewinder	Air-to-air missile	1993	..	..	*For F/A-18D FGA aircraft*
S: Italy	2	Assad Class	Corvette	1995	..	..	*Originally built for Iraq but embargoed*
S: Italy	(12)	Aspide	ShAM	1995	..	..	*For 2 Assad Class corvettes; for use with Albatros Mk-2 ShAM system*
S: Italy	(24)	Otomat Mk-2	ShShM	1995	..	..	*For 2 Assad Class corvettes*
S: Italy	2	RAN-12L/X	Surveillance radar	1995	..	..	*On 2 Assad Class corvettes*
S: Italy	4	RTN-10X	Fire control radar	1995	..	..	*On 2 Assad Class corvettes*
S: Italy	2	Assad Class	Corvette	1996	..	..	*Originally built for Iraq but embargoed*
S: Italy	(12)	Aspide	ShAM	1996	..	..	*For 2 Assad Class corvettes; for use with Albatros Mk-2 ShAM system*
S: Italy	(24)	Otomat Mk-2	ShShM	1996	..	..	*For 2 Assad Class corvettes*
S: Italy	2	RAN-12L/X	Surveillance radar	1996	..	..	*On 2 Assad Class corvettes*
S: Italy	4	RTN-10X	Fire control radar	1996	..	..	*On 2 Assad Class corvettes*
Myanmar							
S: USA	18	Bell-205/UH-1H	Helicopter	(1975)	1975	18	Ex-US Army; gift under International Narcotics Control Program
S: Italy	12	SF-260W Warrior	Trainer aircraft	1975	1975–76	(12)	
S: Netherlands	1	F-27-100 Friendship	Transport aircraft	(1975)	1976	1	
S: USA	(5)	T-37C	Jet trainer aircraft	(1975)	1976	(5)	

S:	No. ordered	Designation	Description	Year of order	Year(s) of delivery	No. delivered	Comments
		Porter					
S: Japan	2	Sinde Class	Landing craft	(1975)	1978	2	
S: USA	5	FH-227 Friendship	Transport aircraft	1978	1978	5	Second-hand; refurbished in Thailand before delivery
S: Switzerland	8	PC-7 Turbo Trainer	Trainer aircraft	1977	1978–79	(8)	
S: Switzerland	(26)	PC-7 Turbo Trainer	Trainer aircraft	1979	1979–81	(26)	
S: Italy	9	SF-260M	Trainer aircraft	1979	1980	(9)	
S: Denmark	3	Osprey Type	Patrol craft	(1978)	1980–82	3	Status uncertain
S: Italy	3	SF-260M	Trainer aircraft	(1981)	1981	3	For VIP transport
S: USA	1	Citation-2	Transport aircraft	1981	1982	1	
S: France	4	SA-342L Gazelle	Helicopter	(1982)	1982–84	4	Second-hand; for VIP transport
S: USA	1	F-27E	Transport aircraft	(1983)	1983	1	Status uncertain
S: Italy	(4)	SF-260M	Trainer aircraft	(1984)	1985	(4)	Original order for 11 reduced to 4
S: Switzerland	4	PC-9	Trainer aircraft	1985	1986	4	
S: China	(55)	Type-63	Light tank	1989	1989–90	(55)	
S: China	12	F-7M Airguard	Fighter aircraft	1990	1990–91	12	Incl. 2 FT-7 fighter/trainer aircraft
S: China	(30)	Type 69-II	Main battle tank	(1989)	1990	(30)	
S: *China*	72	*PL-2B*	*Air-to-air missile*	1990	1990–91	(72)	*For 12 F-7M/FT-7 fighter aircraft*
S: Switzerland	3	PC-9	Trainer aircraft	1990	1990	3	
S: Poland	(6)	Mi-2 Hoplite	Helicopter	(1991)	1991	(6)	
S: Poland	(12)	W-3 Sokol	Helicopter	1990	1991	(12)	
S: China	(200)	HN-5A	Portable SAM	(1991)	1991–92	(200)	
S: Yugoslavia	20	G-4 Super Galeb	Jet trainer aircraft	1990	1991–92	12	Only 12 delivered before destruction of manufacturer in Yugoslav civil war
S: China	10	Hainan Class	Patrol craft	1990	1991–93	10	
S: China	4	Y-8D	Transport aircraft	(1991)	1992–93	(4)	
S: China	10	F-7M Airguard	Fighter aircraft	(1992)	1993	12	Incl. 2 FT-7 fighter/trainer aircraft
S: *China*	(72)	*PL-2B*	*Air-to-air missile*	1992	1993	(72)	*For 12 F-7M/FT-7 fighter aircraft*
S: China	150	Type YW-531H	APC	1993	1993	(150)	

Recipient/ supplier (S) or licenser (L)	No. ordered	Weapon designation	Weapon description	Year of order/ licence	Year(s) of deliveries	No. delivered/ produced	Comments
S: China	(50)	Type-63	Light tank	(1993)	1993	(50)	
S: China	1	JY-8A	Fire control radar	1992	1993	1	For use with 12 Type-59 57-mm AA guns
S: China	(2)	Type-311	Fire control radar	(1993)	1993	(2)	For 24 Type 74 twin 37-mm AA guns; designation uncertain
S: China	(4)	Type-311	Fire control radar	(1993)	1993	(4)	
S: China	(30)	Type-63 107-mm	MRL	(1993)	1993	(30)	
S: China	24	A-5C Fantan	FGA aircraft	(1992)	1995–96	(24)	*For 24 A-5C FGA aircraft*
S: *China*	*(144)*	*PL-2B*	*Air-to-air missile*	*1992*	*1995–96*	*(144)*	
S: China	12	F-7M Airguard	Fighter aircraft	(1993)	1995	(12)	Incl. 2 FT-7 fighter/trainer aircraft
S: *China*	*(72)*	*PL-2B*	*Air-to-air missile*	*1993*	*1995*	*(72)*	*For 12 F-7M/FT-7 fighter aircraft*
S: China	(50)	Type 69-II	Main battle tank	1993	1995	(50)	
S: China	6	Hainan Class	Patrol craft	1994		..	

Singapore

Recipient/ supplier (S) or licenser (L)	No. ordered	Weapon designation	Weapon description	Year of order/ licence	Year(s) of deliveries	No. delivered/ produced	Comments
L: FRG	2	TNC-45 Type	FAC(M)	1970	1975–76	2	Singaporean designation Sea Wolf Class
S: *Israel*	*(20)*	*Gabriel-1*	*ShShM*	*(1970)*	*1975–76*	*(20)*	*For 2 TNC-45 Type (Sea Wolf Class) FAC(M)s*
S: *Netherlands*	*2*	*WM-28*	*Fire control radar*	*(1970)*	*1975–76*	*(6)*	*For 2 TNC-45 Type (Sea Wolf Class) FAC(M)s*
S: South Yemen	5	Jet Provost T-Mk-52	Jet trainer aircraft	1974	1975	5	Ex-South Yemeni Air Force
S: South Yemen	4	BAC-167 Strikemaster	Jet trainer aircraft	1975	1975	4	Ex-South Yemeni Air Force; Mk-81 version
S: USA	2	Bluebird Class	Minesweeper	1975	1975	2	Ex-US Navy; Singaporean designation Jupiter Class
S: India	(63)	Centurion Mk-7	Main battle tank	1975	1975	(63)	Ex-Indian Army

S:	No.	Weapon designation	Description	Order	Delivery	No. del.	Comments
USA	(250)	M-113A1	APC	(1974)	1975–76	(250)	
USA	7	A-4B Skyhawk	FGA aircraft	1972	1975–77	7	Ex-US Navy; refurbished to TA-4S FGA/trainer aircraft before delivery
USA	5	LST-511 Class	Landing ship	1976	1976	5	Ex-US Navy; Singaporean designation Endurance Class
Jordan	2	C-130B Hercules	Transport aircraft	(1976)	1977	2	Ex-Jordanian Air Force
Israel	.(20)	M-71 155-mm	Towed gun	1976	1977	(20)	
USA	(20)	M-114A1 155-mm	Towed gun	(1976)	1977	(20)	Probably ex-US Army
Oman	5	BAC-167 Strikemaster	Jet trainer aircraft	1977	1977	5	Ex-Omani Air Force
USA	2	C-130B Hercules	Transport aircraft	(1977)	1977	2	Ex-US Air Force
USA	17	Bell-205/UH-1H	Helicopter	1977	1977–78	(17)	Deal worth $20 m. incl. 3 Bell 212 helicopters
USA	3	Bell-212	Helicopter	1977	1977–78	(3)	Deal worth $20 m. incl. 17 Bell 205/UH-1H helicopters; for SAR and VIP transport
USA	21	F-5E Tiger-2	FGA aircraft	1976	1979	21	Deal worth $113.2 m. incl. 3 F-5F FGA/trainer aircraft
USA	*200*	*AIM-9J1 Sidewinder*	*Air-to-air missile*	*1976*	*1979*	*200*	*Deal worth $113.2 m. incl. 200 AIM-9J1 missiles; incl. 3 F-5F FGA/trainer aircraft 21 F-5E/F FGA aircraft*
Italy	6	SF-260W Warrior	Trainer aircraft	1979	1979	6	
USA	*200*	*AIM-9P Sidewinder*	*Air-to-air missile*	*1978*	*1979–80*	*200*	
USA	(250)	M-113A1	APC	(1978)	1979–80	(250)	
USA	4	C-130H Hercules	Transport aircraft	(1978)	1980	4	Ex-French Air Force
France	12	T-33A T-Bird	Jet trainer aircraft	1979	1980	12	Ex-US Army; incl. 10 for spares
USA	30	Bell-204/UH-1B	Helicopter	1980	1980	30	Ex-US Navy; some 40 refurbished to A-4S1 in Singapore
USA	70	A-4C Skyhawk	FGA/trainer aircraft	1980	1980–81	(70)	Ex-US Navy; incl. some 40 refurbished to A-4S1 in Singapore and some 30 for spares only

Recipient/ supplier (S) or licenser (L)	No. ordered	Weapon designation	Weapon description	Year of order/ licence	Year(s) of deliveries	No. delivered/ produced	Comments
S: Sweden	(500)	RBS-70	Portable SAM	(1978)	1980–81	(500)	Deal worth $13 m. incl. 25 launchers; incl. assembly in Singapore
S: France	150	AMX-13-90	Light tank	1978	1980–84	(150)	Ex-French Army
S: USA	(8)	M-728	AEV	1980	1981	(8)	Ex-US Army
S: Sweden	(2)	Giraffe-40	Surveillance radar	1978	1982	(2)	
S: USA	6	F-5E Tiger-2	FGA aircraft	1980	1981	6	Deal worth $33.8 m.
S: USA	200	AGM-65A Maverick	ASM	1981	1981	(200)	Deal worth $26 m.
S: Italy	6	SF-260W Warrior	Trainer aircraft	1982	1982	6	
S: UK	6	Blindfire	Fire control radar	1981	1982–83	(6)	For use with 12 Rapier SAM systems
S: USA	(200)	M-113A1	APC	(1981)	1982–83	(200)	
S: UK	12	Rapier SAMS	SAM system	1981	1982–83	(12)	Deal worth $60 m. incl. missiles
S: UK	(204)	Rapier	SAM	1981	1982–83	(204)	For 12 Rapier SAM systems; deal worth $60 m. incl. 12 Rapier SAM systems
S: France	8	T-33A T-Bird	Jet trainer aircraft	1982	1982–83	(8)	Ex-French Air Force
S: France	6	AS-350B Ecureuil	Helicopter	1982	1983	6	For training
S: France	1	AS-350B Ecureuil	Helicopter	1983	1983	1	For training
S: USA	3	F-5F Tiger-2	FGA/trainer aircraft	(1981)	1983	3	Deal worth $16.3 m.
S: Canada	2	Bell-205A-1	Helicopter	(1983)	1983–84	(2)	Second-hand
S: USA	(200)	AIM-9P Sidewinder	Air-to-air missile	(1982)	1983	(200)	Deal worth $12 m.
S: USA	16	TA-4B Skyhawk	FGA/trainer aircraft	1983	1984	(16)	Ex-US Navy; incl. 8 refurbished to TA-4S1 in Singapore and 8 for spares only
S: Bangladesh	2	Bell-205/AB-205	Helicopter	1984	1984	2	Ex-Bangladeshi Air Force
S: Kuwait	4	Bell-205/AB-205	Helicopter	1984	1984	4	Ex-Kuwaiti Air Force; refurbished in Singapore before delivery

		No. ordered	Weapon designation	Weapon description	Year of order	Year(s) of deliveries	No. delivered	Comments
S:	Italy	24	S-211	Jet trainer aircraft	1983	1985–87	(24)	of 24 Deal worth $60 m. incl. 6 direct delivered; assembled from kits
S:	USA	(3)	I-HAWK SAMS	SAM system	(1982)	1985	(3)	For 3 I-HAWK SAM systems
S:	USA	(162)	MIM-23B HAWK	SAM	(1982)	1985	(162)	Prior to licensed production of 17; incl. for SAR
S:	France	5	AS-332B Super Puma	Helicopter	1984	1985	5	
S:	USA	6	F-5E Tiger-2	FGA aircraft	(1984)	1985	6	
S:	USA	24	M-167 Vulcan	AAA system	(1984)	1985–86	(24)	Deal worth $30 m.
L:	France	17	AS-332B Super Puma	Helicopter	1984	1986–88	(17)	Incl. for SAR
S:	USA	3	F-5F Tiger-2	FGA/trainer aircraft	1987	1987	3	
S:	USA	2	C-130H Hercules	Transport aircraft	(1987)	1987	2	
S:	USA	4	E-2C Hawkeye	AEW&C aircraft	1983	1987–88	4	Deal worth $437 m.
S:	USA	8	F-16A Fighting Falcon	FGA aircraft	1985	1988	8	'Peace Carven I' programme worth $280 m.; incl. 4 F-16B FGA/trainer aircraft
S:	USA	(32)	AGM-65D Maverick	ASM	1985	1988	(32)	For 8 F-16A/B FGA aircraft
S:	USA	(48)	AIM-9P Sidewinder	Air-to-air missile	1985	1988	(48)	For 8 F-16A/B FGA aircraft
S:	USA	1	KC-130H Hercules	Tanker aircraft	1988	1988	1	
S:	USA	(48)	RGM-84A Harpoon	ShShM	(1987)	1988–91	(48)	For 6 refitted TNC-45 Type (Sea Wolf Class) FAC(M)s
S:	USA	5	F-5E Tiger-2	FGA aircraft	1988	1989	5	
S:	France	6	AS-332B Super Puma	Helicopter	(1988)	1990	6	Incl. for SAR
S:	USA	24	A-4B Skyhawk	FGA aircraft	1989	1990	24	Ex-US Navy; refurbished to A-4S1 in Singapore
S:	USA	3	AN/TPQ-37	Tracking radar	1989	1990	3	Deal worth $31 m.

Recipient/ supplier (S) or licenser (L)	No. ordered	Weapon designation	Weapon description	Year of order/ licence	Year(s) of deliveries	No. delivered/ produced	Comments
S: FRG	1	Type-62-001	Corvette	1986	1990	1	Prior to licensed production of 5; Singaporean designation Victory Class
L: FRG	5	Type-62-001	Corvette	1986	1990–91	5	Singaporean designation Victory Class
S: USA	(96)	RGM-84A Harpoon	ShShM	(1986)	1990–91	(96)	For 6 Type-62-001 (Victory Class) corvettes
S: Sweden	6	Sea Giraffe-150	Surveillance radar	(1986)	1990—91	(6)	For 6 Type-62-001 (Victory Class) corvettes
S: France	(200)	Milan-2	Anti-tank missile	1989	1990–92	(200)	Deal incl. also 30 launchers
S: France	10	AS-550A2 Fennec	Helicopter	1990	1991	(10)	Assembled in Singapore
S: France	22	AMX-10P	AIFV	(1990)	1991–92	(22)	
S: France	37	LG-1 105-mm	Towed gun	1990	1991–93	(37)	
S: France	10	AS-550C2 Fennec	Combat helicopter	(1990)	1992	(10)	Assembled in Singapore
S: USA	(400)	BGM-71C I-TOW	Anti-tank missile	(1990)	1992	(400)	For 10 AS-550C2 helicopters
S: Italy	(1)	Skyguard	Fire control radar	1991	1992	(1)	For use with GDF-002 35-mm anti-aircraft gun
S: France	22	AMX-10/PAC-90	AIFV	1990	1992	(22)	
S: South Africa	1	Lancelot Class	Landing ship	1992	1992	1	Former British Navy landing ship bought from civilian company; Singaporean designation Perseverance Class
S: USA	(48)	MIM-23B HAWK	SAM	1991	1993	(48)	
S: USA	9	F-16A Fighting Falcon	FGA aircraft	1992	1993	9	Ex-US Air Force; 3-year lease; incl. 2 F-16B FGA/trainer aircraft
S: USA	20	AGM-84A Harpoon	Air-to-ship missile	1991	1993–94	(20)	For 5 F-50 Maritime Enforcer aircraft
S: Jordan	7	F-5E Tiger-2	FGA aircraft	1994	1994	7	Ex-Jordanian Air Force; deal worth $21 m.
S: France	(20)	AMX-10P	AIFV	(1993)	1994	20	
S: Netherlands	4	Fokker-50 Utility	Transport aircraft	1994	1994	(4)	

Supplier	No.	Weapon designation	Weapon description	Year of order	Year of delivery	No. delivered	Comments
		Enforcer-2					
S: France	150	Mistral	Portable SAM	1992	1994–95	(150)	Deal incl. 30 launchers; incl. for navy
S: UK	(18)	FV-180 CET	AEV	1993	1994–95	(18)	
S: Sweden	4	Landsort Class	MCM ship	1991	1995	4	Incl. 3 assembled from kits in Singapore; Singaporean designation Bedok Class
S: Israel	*(96)*	*Barak*	*ShAM*	*(1992)*	*1996*	*(16)*	*For 6 Victory Class corvettes*
S: USA	6	CH-47D Chinook	Helicopter	1994	1996	(6)	Incl. 3 for SAR
S: Sweden	1	Sjöormen Class	Submarine	1995	1996	1	Ex-Swedish Navy; refitted before delivery; for training
S: USA	18	F-16D Fighting Falcon	FGA aircraft	1994		..	'Peace Carven II' programme worth $890 m. incl. 50 AIM-7M and 36 AIM-9S missiles; incl. 8 F-16C
							FGA/trainer aircraft
S: USA	*50*	*AIM-7M Sparrow*	*Air-to-air missile*	*1994*		..	*Deal worth $890 m incl. 18 F-16C/D*
							FGA aircraft and 36 AIM-9S missiles
S: USA	*30*	*AIM-9S Sidewinder*	*Air-to-air missile*	*1994*		..	*Deal worth $890 m incl. 18 F-16C/D*
							FGA aircraft and 50 AIM-7M missiles
S: USA	*24*	*AGM-84A Harpoon*	*Air-to-ship missile*	*1996*		..	*Deal worth $39 m.; for Fokker-50 ASW/MP aircraft*
S: USA	(2)	LPD Type	AALS	1994		..	Designed for production in Singapore; option on 2 more
S: UK	18	FV-180 CET	AEV	1995		..	
Thailand							
S: USA	4	EC-47	EW aircraft	(1974)	1975	4	Ex-US Air Force
S: Israel	(20)	M-68 155-mm	Towed gun	(1974)	1975	(20)	Status uncertain
S: Israel	(24)	M-68 155-mm	Towed gun	(1974)	1975	(24)	
S: USA	2	LST-511 Class	Landing ship	(1975)	1975	2	Ex-US Navy
S: USA	20	AU-23A	CAS/COIN aircraft	1974	1975–76	20	Deal worth $12 m.; incl. 5 for police

Recipient/ supplier (S) or licenser (L)	No. ordered	Weapon designation	Weapon description	Year of order/ licence	Year(s) of deliveries	No. delivered/ produced	Comments
S: UK	1	BN-2A Islander	Light transport plane	(1974)	1976	1	
S: USA	50	M-48A3 Paton	Main battle tank	(1975)	1976	50	
S: Italy	(1)	PLUTO	Surveillance radar	(1975)	1976	(1)	
S: Singapore	3	TNC-45 Type	FAC(M)	1973	1976–77	3	Thai designation Prabparapak Class
S: Israel	(45)	Gabriel-1	ShShM	1973	1976–77	(45)	For 3 TNC-45 Type (*Prabparapak Class*) FAC(M)s
S: Netherlands	3	WM-28	Fire control radar	(1973)	1976–77	(3)	For 3 TNC-45 Type (*Prabparapak Class*) FAC(M)s
S: USA	13	Bell-205/UH-1H	Helicopter	(1976)	1977	13	
S: Switzerland	5	PC-7 Turbo Trainer	Trainer aircraft	1976	1977	5	
S: UK	20	Saracen	APC	(1976)	1977	(20)	Ex-British Army
S: USA	2	Bell-212	Helicopter	1977	1977	2	For army; for VIP transport
S: USA	2	Merlin-4	Transport aircraft	1977	1977–78	2	
S: USA	20	F-5E Tiger-2	FGA aircraft	1976	1978	20	Deal worth $80 m.; incl. 3 F-5F FGA/trainer aircraft
S: USA	(120)	AIM-9J Sidewinder	Air-to-air missile	1976	1978	(120)	For 20 F-5E/F FGA aircraft
S: Canada	2	CL-215	Transport aircraft	1977	1978	2	For navy; for SAR
S: USA	18	S-58/UH-34	Helicopter	1977	1978	18	Second-hand
S: USA	2	Bell-214B BigLifter	Helicopter	1978	1978	2	For army
S: UK	154	Scorpion	Light tank	1977	1978–84	(154)	
S: USA	4	CH-47A Chinook	Helicopter	1978	1979	4	Ex-US Army; for army
S: USA	47	M-108 105-mm	Self-propelled gun	1978	1979	47	Ex-US Army
S: USA	3	Merlin-4	Transport aircraft	1978	1979	3	
S: Italy	3	MV-250 Type	FAC(M)	1976	1979–80	3	Thai designation Ratcharit Class

								FAC(M)s
S:	*France*	*(24)*	*MM-38 Exocet*	*ShShM*	*(1976)*	*1979–80*	*(24)*	*For 3 MV-250 Type (Ratcharit Class) FAC(M)s*
S:	USA	215	BGM-71A TOW	Anti-tank missile	1978	1980	215	Deal incl. also 12 launchers
S:	Indonesia	1	CN-212-100 Aviocar	Transport aircraft	(1978)	1980	1	
L:	FRG	1	Thalang Class	MCM ship	(1978)	1980	1	Designed for production in Thailand
S:	USA	1	Beech-99A Airliner	Transport aircraft	(1979)	1980	1	For army
S:	USA	3	C-130H Hercules	Transport aircraft	1979	1980	3	Deal worth $47.7 m.
S:	USA	600	FGM-77A Dragon	Anti-tank missile	(1979)	1980	600	
S:	USA	30	M-113A1	APC	(1979)	1980	30	Ex-US Army
S:	USA	6	T-37B	Jet trainer aircraft	(1979)	1980	6	Ex-US Air Force; deal worth $1.4 m.
S:	USA	40	M-113A1	APC	1980	1980	40	
S:	USA	14	Bell-205/UH-1A	Helicopter	1977	1980–81	14	For army
S:	USA	34	M-114A1 155-mm	Towed gun	1979	1980–81	(34)	
S:	USA	55	M-48A5 Patton	Main battle tank	(1979)	1980–81	(55)	
S:	USA	2	AN/TPS-43	Surveillance radar	(1980)	1980–81	(2)	
S:	USA	24	M-163 Vulcan	AAV(G)	1980	1980–81	(24)	
S:	Israel	3	IAI-201 Arava	Light transport plane	1980	1980–82	3	For survey and ECM roles
S:	USA	(164)	Commando V-150	APC	1978	1980–83	(164)	
S:	USA	20	F-5E Tiger-2	FGA aircraft	1979	1981	20	Incl. 3 F-5F FGA/trainer aircraft
S:	*USA*	*239*	*AIM-9P Sidewinder*	*Air-to-air missile*	*(1979)*	*1981*	*239*	*For F-5E/F FGA aircraft*
S:	USA	24	M-101A1 105-mm	Towed gun	1979	1981	(24)	
S:	USA	6	Cessna-337/O-2	Light transport plane	1980	1981	6	Ex-US Air Force; refurbished before delivery; for navy
S:	USA	2	Queen Air-A65	Light transport plane	(1980)	1981	(2)	
S:	Austria	12	GC-45 155-mm	Towed gun	1981	1981	12	
S:	USA	2	Bell-412	Helicopter	1981	1982	2	

Recipient/ supplier (S) or licenser (L)	No. ordered	Weapon designation	Weapon description	Year of order/ licence	Year(s) of deliveries	No. delivered/ produced	Comments
S: UK	(100)	Blowpipe	Portable SAM	1981	1982	(100)	Bought after US refusal to supply FIM-43A SAMs; for air force
S: USA	20	FIM-43A Redeye	Portable SAM	(1981)	1982	20	
S: Italy	6	SF-260M	Trainer	(1981)	1982	(6)	
S: USA	12	Bell-205/UH-1H	Helicopter	1982	1982	12	For army; deal worth $30 m.
S: Malaysia	2	F-5B Freedom Fighter	FGA/trainer aircraft	1982	1982	2	Ex-Malaysian Air Force
S: USA	24	M-167 Vulcan	AAA system	1982	1982	24	
S: Australia	20	N-22B Missionmaster	Transport aircraft	1981	1982–84	(20)	Deal worth $33 m.
S: Italy	2	MV-400 Type	Patrol craft	1979	1983	2	Thai designation Chon Buri Class
S: USA	1	C-130H-30 Hercules	Transport aircraft	1981	1983	1	
S: UK	(50)	Blowpipe	Portable SAM	1982	1983	(50)	For air force
S: USA	2	LA-4-200	Light aircraft	(1982)	1983	(2)	For navy
S: USA	18	M-198 155-mm	Towed gun	1982	1983	18	Deal worth $17 m.
S: France	12	T-33A T-Bird	Jet trainer aircraft	1982	1983	12	Ex-French Air Force; refurbished before delivery
S: USA	4	T-37B	Jet trainer aircraft	(1983)	1983	4	Ex-US Air Force
S: USA	(100)	FIM-43A Redeye	Portable SAM	1983	1983	(100)	
S: Netherlands	(12)	Flycatcher	Fire control radar	(1982)	1983–84	(12)	
S: Netherlands	3	WM-22	Fire control radar	(1979)	1983–84	(3)	For 3 MV-400 Type (Chon Buri Class) patrol craft
S: USA	34	M-114A1 155-mm	Towed gun	1982	1983–84	(34)	
S: Italy	1	MV-400 Type	Patrol craft	1981	1984	1	Thai designation Chon Buri Class
S: UK	(50)	Blowpipe	Portable SAM	1982	1984	(50)	Deal worth $1.7 m.; for air force

S:	FRG	2	Enforcer Fantrainer	Trainer aircraft	1982	1984	2	Prior to licensed production
S:	USA	1	Boeing-737-200L	Transport aircraft	(1983)	1984	1	For VIP transport with Royal Flight
S:	USA	44	M-198 155-mm	Towed gun	(1983)	1984	(44)	
S:	Australia	4	N-22L Searchmaster	MP aircraft	1983	1984	(4)	For navy
S:	USA	1	Super King Air-200	Transport aircraft	(1983)	1984	1	
S:	USA	2	Bell-214ST	Helicopter	1984	1984	2	
S:	USA	4	Cessna-337/O-2	Light transport plane	(1984)	1984	4	Ex-US Air Force; refurbished before delivery; for navy
S:	FRG	1	M-41 Walker Bulldog	Light tank	1984	1984	1	Ex-FRG Army; refurbished before delivery; for trials
S:	USA	(9)	AN/TPQ-36	Tracking radar	1982	1984–85	(9)	
S:	UK	4	Shorts-330UTT	Transport aircraft	1982	1984–85	(4)	Incl. 2 for army and 2 for border police
S:	France	10	MM-40 CDS	Coast defence system	(1983)	1984–85	(10)	
S:	France	(60)	MM-40 Exocet	CShM	(1983)	1984–85	(60)	For 10 MM-40 coast defence systems
S:	USA	21	LVTP-7A1	APC	1984	1984–85	(21)	
S:	USA	40	M-48A5 Patton	Main battle tank	1984	1984–85	(40)	
S:	USA	148	M-113A2	APC	1982	1984–86	(148)	
S:	USA	1	AN/TPS-43	Surveillance radar	1984	1985	1	
S:	USA	(8)	Bell-212	Helicopter	(1984)	1985	(8)	
S:	USA	43	Dragoon-300	APC	1984	1985	43	For army
S:	USA	(20)	M-198 155-mm	Towed gun	1984	1985	(20)	
S:	Australia	1	N-22L Searchmaster	MP aircraft	1984	1985	(1)	For navy; for anti-piracy patrols; financed by UNHCR
S:	USA	7	Bell-206B JetRanger-3	Helicopter	1985	1985	7	
S:	Australia	4	N-22L Searchmaster	MP aircraft	(1985)	1985	4	For navy; aid

Recipient/ supplier (S) or licenser (L)	No. ordered	Weapon designation	Weapon description	Year of order/ licence	Year(s) of deliveries	No. delivered/ produced	Comments
S: China	18	Type-59-1 130-mm	Towed gun	(1985)	1985	18	Gift
S: China	24	Type-59	Main battle tank	(1985)	1985	24	Gift
S: Indonesia	3	CN-212-100 Aviocar	Transport aircraft	1985	1985–86	(3)	
S: Singapore	20	T-33A T-Bird	Jet trainer aircraft	(1985)	1986	20	Ex-Singapore Air Force; incl. some for spares only
S: USA	24	Hughes-300C	Helicopter	(1986)	1986	(24)	For training
S: China	6	Type-59	Main battle tank	(1986)	1986	(6)	Probably ARV version
S: USA	2	Rattanakosin Class	Corvette	1983	1986–87	2	Deal worth $144 m.
S: Italy	(48)	Aspide	ShAM	1984	1986–87	(48)	For 2 Rattanakosin Class corvettes
S: Netherlands	2	DA-05	Surveillance radar	(1983)	1986–87	(2)	For 2 Rattanakosin Class corvettes
S: USA	(32)	RGM-84A Harpoon	ShShM	1983	1986–87	(32)	For 2 Rattanakosin Class corvettes
S: Netherlands	2	WM-25	Fire control radar	(1983)	1986–87	(2)	For 2 Rattanakosin Class corvettes
S: USA	4	AN/TPQ-37	Tracking radar	1985	1986–87	(4)	
S: USA	10	Cessna-208	Light transport plane	1985	1986–87	(10)	For army
L: FRG	45	Fantrainer	Trainer aircraft	1983	1986–91	(45)	
S: FRG	2	M-40 Type	Minesweeper	1984	1987	2	Deal worth $36 m.; Thai designation Bang Rachan Class; option on 2 more not used
L: France	1	PS-700 Class	Landing ship	1984	1987	(1)	
S: Netherlands	1	F-27 Maritime Enforcer	ASW/MP aircraft	1985	1987	1	For navy
S: USA	4	LAADS	Surveillance radar	1985	1987	(4)	Deal worth $17.5 m.
S: USA	(2)	AN/MPQ-4	Tracking radar	(1986)	1987	(2)	
S: Netherlands	2	F-27-400M	Transport plane	1986	1987	2	For navy

S	Weapon designation	Weapon description	No. ordered	Year of order	Year of deliveries	No. delivered	Comments
China	Type-59-1 130-mm	Towed gun	(18)	(1986)	1987	18	
USA	Bell-214ST	Helicopter	5	(1987)	1987	(5)	For navy
China	HN-5A	Portable SAM	(50)	1987	1987	(50)	
China	Type-69	Main battle tank	30	(1987)	1987	(30)	
China	Type YW-531	APC	410	1987	1987	410	
Italy	Fieldguard	Fire control radar	(24)	(1987)	1987–88	(24)	
USA	M-48A5 Patton	Main battle tank	40	1987	1987–88	(40)	For use with 30-mm AA guns
Italy	Skyguard	Fire control radar	2	1987	1987–89	2	'Peace Naresuan' programme worth $378 m.; incl. 4 F-16B FGA/trainer aircraft
USA	F-16A Fighting Falcon	FGA aircraft	12	1985	1988	12	
USA	*AGM-65D Maverick*	*ASM*	*(48)*	*1985*	*1988*	*(48)*	*For 12 F-16A/B FGA aircraft*
USA	*AIM-9P Sidewinder*	*Air-to-air missile*	*(96)*	*(1985)*	*1988*	*(96)*	*For 12 F-16A/B FGA aircraft*
USA	Bell-209/AH-1S	Combat helicopter	4	1986	1988	4	
Italy	Spada SAMS	SAM system	1	1986	1988	1	For 1 Spada SAM system
Italy	*Aspide*	*SAM*	*(36)*	*1986*	*1988*	*(36)*	*For use with 1 Spada SAM system*
Austria	GHN-45 155-mm	Towed gun	6	1987	1988	6	
USA	Learjet-35A	Light transport plane	3	1987	1988	3	
Italy	PLUTO	Surveillance radar	1	(1987)	1988	(1)	
China	Type-81 122-mm	MRL	(36)	(1987)	1988	(36)	
USA	Bell-212	Helicopter	5	1988	1988	5	For VIP transport
USA	F-5E Tiger-2	FGA aircraft	10	1988	1988	(10)	Ex-US Air Force
China	HN-5A	Portable SAM	(18)	1988	1988	(18)	
Israel	M-71 155-mm	Towed gun	(32)	(1988)	1988	(32)	
USA	T-33A T-Bird	Jet trainer aircraft	(6)	1988	1988	(6)	
China	Type-59-1 130-mm	Towed gun	18	1988	1988	(18)	

Recipient/ supplier (S) or licenser (L)	No. ordered	Weapon designation	Weapon description	Year of order/ licence	Year(s) of deliveries	No. delivered/ produced	Comments
S: China	(60)	Type-85 130-mm	MRL	(1988)	1988–89	(60)	
S: USA	(106)	Stingray	Light tank	1987	1988–90	106	Deal worth $150 m.
L: France	1	PS-700 Class	Landing ship	(1985)	1989	1	
S: USA	6	*AGM-84A Harpoon*	*Air-to-ship missile*	1987	1989	6	*For 3 F-27 ASW/MP aircraft*
S: USA	1	Boeing-737-200L	Transport aircraft	(1987)	1989	1	For VIP transport
S: USA	4	CH-47D Chinook	Helicopter	1988	1989	4	
S: China	1	HQ-2B SAMS	SAM system	1988	1989	(1)	
S: China	(12)	*HQ-2B*	*SAM*	1988	1989	(12)	*For 1 HQ-2B SAM system*
S: USA	24	Hughes-300C	Helicopter	1988	1989	24	
S: Italy	(1)	RAT-31S	Surveillance radar	(1988)	1989	(1)	Deal worth $10 m.
S: China	23	Type-69	Main battle tank	1988	1989	(23)	
S: USA	4	Bell-209/AH-1S	Combat helicopter	1988	1989–90	4	*For 4 Bell-209 AH-1S combat helicopters*
S: USA	(320)	*BGM-71D TOW-2*	*Anti-tank missile*	(1988)	1989–90	(320)	
S: USA	3	C-130H-30 Hercules	Transport aircraft	1988	1989–90	3	Deal worth $66 m.
S: China	(450)	Type-69	Main battle tank	1987	1989–92	(450)	
S: USA	10	Bell-205/UH-1A	Helicopter	1989	1990	10	Deal worth $118 m.
S: USA	1	C-130H Hercules	Transport aircraft	(1989)	1990	1	
S: Israel	40	*Python-3*	*Air-to-air missile*	1989	1990	(40)	*For F-16 FGA aircraft*
S: USA	81	M-125A1 81-mm	APC/mortar carrier	1990	1990	(81)	Deal worth $27 m.
S: China	360	Type YW-531	APC	1988	1990–91	(360)	
S: USA	20	MX-7-180	Light aircraft	(1990)	1990–91	(20)	
S: USA	6	F-16A Fighting Falcon	FGA aircraft	1987	1991	6	'Peace Naresuan II' programme

		Maverick					
S: USA	(36)	*AIM-9P Sidewinder*	*Air-to-air missile*	*(1987)*	*1991*	*(36)*	*For 6 F-16A FGA aircraft*
S: USA	2	AN/FPS-117	Surveillance radar	1989	1991	(2)	Deal worth $43 m.
S: USA	3	CH-47D Chinook	Helicopter	1990	1991	3	
S: FRG	3	Do-228-200MP	MP aircraft	1990	1991	3	For navy
S: USA	53	M-60A1 Patton-2	Main battle tank	1990	1991	(53)	Ex-US Army
S: USA	20	M-88A1	ARV	1990	1991	(20)	
S: France	1	Airbus A300	Transport aircraft	(1991)	1991	1	For VIP transport
S: China	4	Jianghu Class	Frigate	1988	1991–92	4	Thai designation Chao Phraya Class
S: China	6	*100-mm L56 Twin Naval gun*		*1988*	*1991–92*	*6*	*For 4 Jianghu (Chao Phraya) Class frigates*
S: China	96	*C-801*	*ShShM*	*1988*	*1991–92*	*(96)*	*Deal worth $40 m.; for 4 Jianghu (Chao Phraya) Class frigates*
S: Switzerland	20	PC-9	Trainer aircraft	1990	1991–92	(20)	Deal worth $90 m. incl. training
S: China	(25)	Type-311	Fire control radar	1991	1991–92	(25)	
S: USA	(2)	AN/TPS-70	Surveillance radar	1985	1992	2	
L: UK	3	Province Class	Patrol craft	1987	1992	3	
S: USA	17	M-113A2	APC	1988	1992	17	Deal worth $63 m. incl. 20 M-109A5 155-mm self-propelled guns, 20 M-992 ALVs and 11 M-577A2 APC/CPs
S: USA	11	M-577A2	APC/CP	1988	1992	(11)	Deal worth $63 m. incl. 20 M-109A5 155-mm self-propelled guns, 20 M-992 ALVs and 17 M-113A3 APCs
L: UK	1	Province Class	Patrol craft	1989	1992	1	For marine police
S: New Zealand	6	CT-4 Airtrainer	Trainer aircraft	(1990)	1992	(6)	
S: Austria	(18)	GHN-45 155-mm	Towed gun	(1991)	1992	18	
S: UK	2	Martello-743D	Surveillance radar	1991	1992	(2)	
S: USA	2	C-130H-30 Hercules	Transport aircraft	1991	1993	(2)	
S: USA	2	C-130H Hercules	Transport aircraft	1992	1993	(2)	

Recipient/ supplier (S) or licenser (L)	No. ordered	Weapon designation	Weapon description	Year of order/ licence	Year(s) of deliveries	No. delivered/ produced	Comments
S: FRG	18	Condor	APC	(1992)	1993	18	Deal worth $19.2 m.
S: USA	20	M-992 FAASV	ALV	1988	1993–94	20	Deal worth $63 m. incl. 20 M-109A5 155-mm self-propelled guns, 17 M-113A3 APCs and 11 M-577A2 APC/CPs
S: Czech Republic	36	L-39Z Albatros	Jet trainer aircraft	1992	1993–94	36	Deal worth $200 m.
S: USA	20	M-109A5 155-mm	Self-propelled gun	(1988)	1994	(20)	Deal worth $63 m. incl. 20 M-992 ALVs, 17 M-113A3 APCs and 11 M-577A2 APC/CPs
S: USA	5	P-3A Orion	ASW/MP aircraft	1993	1994	(5)	Ex-US Navy; incl. 2 for spares only
S: USA	16	AGM-84A Harpoon	Air-to-ship missile	1990	1994	(16)	For 3 P-3B ASW aircraft
S: China	2	Naresuan Class	Frigate	1989	1994–95	2	Weapons and electronics fitted in Thailand
S: USA	2	127-mm/54 Mk-45	Naval gun	(1990)	1994–95	(2)	For 2 Naresuan Class frigates
S: USA	(32)	RGM-84A Harpoon	ShShM	(1991)	1994–95	(32)	For 2 Naresuan Class frigates
S: USA	(48)	RIM-7M Seasparrow	ShAM	(1991)	1994–95	(48)	For 2 Naresuan Class frigates
S: Netherlands	2	LW-08	Surveillance radar	1995	1995	(2)	For 2 Naresuan Class frigates
S: Netherlands	4	STIR	Fire control radar	1992	1994–95	(4)	For 2 Naresuan Class frigates
S: Canada	(4)	ADATS SAMS	SAM system	1993	1994–95	(4)	
S: Canada	(32)	ADATS	SAM	1993	1994–95	(32)	For 4 ADATS SAM systems
S: Italy	6	G-222	Transport aircraft	1994	1994–95	(6)	Deal worth $136 m.; option on 4-6 more
S: USA	2	Knox Class	Frigate	1992	1994–96	(2)	Ex-US Navy; 5-year lease worth $4.3 m.
S: USA	(32)	RGM-84A Harpoon	ShShM	(1991)	1994–96	(32)	For 2 Knox Class frigates
S: USA	2	LAADS	Surveillance radar	1993	1995	(1)	Deal worth $11.8 m.

S:	No.	Designation	Description	Year of order	Year of delivery	No. delivered	Comments
		Falcon					FGA/trainer aircraft
S: USA	6	S-70B/SH-60B Seahawk	ASW helicopter	1993	1995	(1)	Deal worth $186 m.; for navy
S: Austria	18	GHN-45 155-mm	Towed gun	1995	1995	18	For coastguard
S: Spain	2	C-212-200 Aviocar	Transport aircraft	1995	1995	(2)	For army
S: UK	2	Jetstream-41	Transport aircraft	1995	1995	1	Ex-US Army; deal worth $127 m.
S: USA	101	M-60A3 Patton-2	Main battle tank	1995	1995	24	Ex-US Navy; incl. 3 for spares only; deal worth $81.6 m.; incl. 4 TA-7C FGA/trainer aircraft; for navy
S: USA	21	A-7E Corsair-2	FGA aircraft	1994	1995–96	(21)	For navy
S: FRG	3	Do-228-200MP	MP aircraft	1995	1995–96	3	Deal worth $382 m.
S: France	24	LG-1 105-mm	Towed gun	1996	1996	(12)	Deal worth $257 m. without armament and radars
S: USA	3	E-2C Hawkeye	AEW&C aircraft	1991		..	*For 1 Chakri Nareubet Class aircraft-carrier*
S: Spain	1	Chakri Nareubet Class	Aircraft-carrier	1992		..	*For 1 Chakri Nareubet Class aircraft-carrier*
S: USA	*(4)*	*Phalanx*	*CIWS*	*1994*		..	Deal worth $130 m.
S: USA	*(8)*	*RIM-7M Seasparrow*	*ShAM*	*(1996)*		..	For VIP transport
S: Canada	20	Bell-212	Helicopter	1993		..	
S: France	3	AS-332L2 Super Puma	Helicopter	1995		..	
S: Spain	9	Harrier Mk-50/ AV-8A	FGA aircraft	1995		..	Incl. 2 Harrier Mk-54/TAV-8s FGA/trainer aircraft; deal worth $90 m.; for navy
S: USA	12	M-106A3 120-mm	APC/mortar carrier	1995		..	Deal worth $85 m. incl. 70 other M-113A3 versions
S: USA	19	M-113A3	APC	1995		..	Deal worth $85 m. incl. 63 other M-113A3 versions; incl. 9 ambulance, and 10 ARV versions

Recipient/ supplier (S) or licenser (L)	Weapon designation	No. ordered	Weapon description	Year of order/ licence	Year(s) of deliveries	No. delivered/ produced	Comments
S: USA	M-125A3 81-mm	21	APC/mortar carrier	1995	..	..	Deal worth $85 m. incl. 61 other M-113A3 versions
S: USA	M-577A3	12	APC/CP	1995	..	..	Deal worth $85 m. incl. 70 other M-113A3 versions
S: USA	M-901 ITV	18	Tank destroyer (M)	1995	..	..	Deal worth $85 m. incl. 64 other M-113A3 versions
S: USA	S-76/H-76 Eagle	6	Helicopter	1995	..	..	
S: USA	W-2100	3	Surveillance radar	1995	..	..	
Viet Nam							
S: USSR	BM-21 122-mm	(50)	MRL	(1973)	1975	(50)	
S: USSR	SA-7 Grail	(1 500)	Portable SAM	(1978)	1978	(1 500)	
S: USSR	Petya-3 Class	2	Corvette	1978	1978	2	
S: USSR	D-20 152-mm	(500)	Towed gun	(1978)	1978–79	(500)	Status uncertain
S: USSR	T-62	(200)	Main battle tank	(1978)	1978–79	(200)	
S: USSR	ZSU-23-4 Shilka	(100)	AAV(G)	(1978)	1978–79	(100)	
S: USSR	An-12 Cub-A	12	Transport aircraft	(1979)	1979	12	
S: USSR	BTR-60P	(1 000)	APC	(1979)	1979	(1 000)	
S: USSR	Yurka Class	2	Minesweeper	1979	1979	2	Status uncertain
S: USSR	Mi-6 Hook-A	11	Helicopter	1979	1979–80	(11)	Ex-Soviet Navy
S: USSR	Mi-8 Hip-C	(30)	Helicopter	1979	1979–80	(30)	Ex-Soviet Air Force
S: USSR	Polnocny Class	3	Landing ship	(1979)	1979–80	3	Ex-Soviet Navy
S: USSR	SA-6 SAMS	(10)	SAM system	(1979)	1979–80	(10)	
S: *USSR*	*SA-6 Gainful*	(200)	SAM	(1979)	*1979–80*	(200)	*For 10 SA-6 SAM systems*
S: USSR	Ka-25 Hormone-A	(15)	ASW helicopter	1979	1979–81	(15)	For navy

	No.	Designation	Category	(Year of order)	Year(s) of delivery	(No. delivered)	Comments
		Fishbed-C					
S: USSR	(60)	MiG-21bis Fishbed-N	Fighter aircraft	(1979)	1979–81	(60)	
S: USSR	8	Osa-2 Class	FAC(M)	(1979)	1979–81	8	Ex-Soviet Navy
S: USSR	*(48)*	*SS-N-2b Styx*	*ShShM*	*(1979)*	*1979–81*	*(48)*	*For 8 Osa-2 Class FAC(M)s*
S: USSR	14	Shershen Class	FAC(T)	(1979)	1979–83	14	
S: Czechoslovakia	24	L-39C Albatros	Jet trainer aircraft	(1980)	1980–81	24	
S: USSR	8	SO-1 Class	Patrol craft	(1979)	1980–83	8	Ex-Soviet Navy
S: USSR	(70)	Su-20 Fitter-C	FGA aircraft	(1980)	1981	(70)	For navy
S: USSR	(6)	Be-12 Mail	ASW/MP aircraft	(1981)	1982–83	(6)	Status uncertain
S: USSR	30	Mi-8 Hip-E	Helicopter	(1982)	1982–84	(30)	
S: USSR	(10)	SA-3 SAMS	SAM system	(1983)	1983	(10)	
S: USSR	*(220)*	*SA-3b Goa*	*SAM*	*(1983)*	*1983*	*(220)*	*For 10 SA-3 SAM systems*
S: USSR	(51)	MiG-21F Fishbed-C	Fighter aircraft	(1982)	1983	(51)	Ex-Soviet Air Force
S: USSR	50	An-26 Curl-A	Transport aircraft	1979	1983–84	(50)	
S: USSR	3	Petya-2 Class	Corvette	1983	1983–84	3	Ex-Soviet Navy
S: USSR	(2)	AN-30 Clank	Recce aircraft	(1983)	1984	(2)	
S: USSR	2	Ka-25 Hormone-A	ASW helicopter	(1984)	1984	(2)	For navy; status uncertain
S: USSR	30	Mi-24 Hind-D	Combat helicopter	(1984)	1984–85	(30)	
S: USSR	5	Turya Class	FAC(T)	(1983)	1984–86	5	
S: USSR	(30)	MiG-23MF Flogger-E	Fighter aircraft	(1985)	1986–87	(30)	
S: USSR	4	Sonya Class	MCM ship	1987	1987–90	4	
S: Russia	6	Su-27 Flanker	FGA aircraft	(1994)	1995	6	Deal worth $200 m.
S: Russia	*(108)*	*AA-10a Alamo*	*Air-to-air missile*	*(1994)*	*1995*	*(108)*	*For 6 Su-27 fighters; may incl. other AA-10 versions*
S: Russia	*(72)*	*AA-11 Archer*	*Air-to-air missile*	*(1994)*	*1995*	*(72)*	*For 6 Su-27 fighters*
S: Russia	2	Tarantul-1 Class	FAC(M)	1994		..	

Recipient/ supplier (S) or licenser (L)	No. ordered	Weapon designation	Weapon description	Year of order/ licence	Year(s) of deliveries	No. delivered/ produced	Comments
S: Russia	(80)	SA-N-5 Grail	ShAM	1995		..	For 2 Tarantul-1 Class FAC(M)s
S: Russia	(16)	SS-N-2d Styx	ShShM	1995		..	For 2 Tarantul-1 Class FAC(M)s

Acronyms and abbreviations

(M)	Missile-armed
(T)	Torpedo-armed
AA	Anti-aircraft
AAA	Anti-aircraft artillery
AALS	Amphibious assault landing ship
AAV(G)	Anti-aircraft vehicle (gun-armed)
AEV	Armoured engineer vehicle
AIFV	Armoured infantry fighting vehicle
ALV	Armoured logistic vehicle
APC	Armoured personnel carrier
APC/CP	Armoured personnel carrier/command post
ARV	Armoured recovery vehicle
AShM	Air-to-ship missile
ASM	Air-to-surface missile
ASW	Anti-submarine warfare
AEW&C	Airborne early warning and control
b.	Billion (10⁹)
C³I	Command, control, communications and intelligence
CAS/COIN	Close air support/counter-insurgency
CIWS	Close-in weapon system
CShM	Coast-to-ship missile
ECM	Electronic countermeasures
ELINT	ELectronic intelligence

EW	Electronic warfare
FAC	Fast attack craft
FGA	Fighter/ground attack (aircraft)
FRG	Federal Republic of Germany
m.	Million (10⁶)
MAP	Military aid programme (US)
MCM	Mine countermeasures
MP	Maritime patrol (aircraft)
MRL	Multiple rocket launcher
OPV	Off-shore patrol vessel
Recce	Reconnaissance
SAM	Surface-to-air missile
SAR	Search and rescue
ShAM	Ship-to-air missile
ShShM	Ship-to-ship missile
UAE	United Arab Emirates
UNHCR	UN High Commissioner for Refugees
VIP	Very important person
VLS	Vertical-launch system (for missiles)

Conventions

( )   Uncertain data/SIPRI estimate
..   Data not available

Source: SIPRI arms transfers database, 1996.

About the contributors

Amitav Acharya (Canada) is currently Senior Research Fellow at the Joint Centre for Asia Pacific Studies, York University, Canada, and was formerly Research Fellow with the Institute for Southeast Asian Studies in Singapore. He is a specialist on ASEAN and East Asian defence issues and has published extensively on the topic, including *Chinese Defense Expenditures: Trends and Implications* (1994); *An Arms Race in Post-Cold War Southeast Asia: Prospects for Control* (1994); and *A New Regional Order in Southeast Asia: ASEAN in the Post-Cold War Era* (1993).

Kang Choi (South Korea) is Associate Research Fellow and Chief of the Division of Arms Control Environment Analysis at the Arms Control Research Centre in the Korea Institute for Defense Analyses, Seoul. He has published extensively on arms control, the arms trade, confidence building and security and his most recent publications include *Negotiation Strategies for Cease-fire and War Termination* (1995); *Prospects for the Implementation of the Agreed Framework* (1995); and *Military Transparency Measures in Northeast Asia* (1994). *Possible Patterns of Chinese Intervention in the Korean Contingencies; The ROK's Position on the Arms Control-Related Resolutions of the United Nations;* and 'Unified Korea's security policy' are forthcoming.

Bates Gill (USA) was until February 1997 Head of the SIPRI Project on Security and Arms Control in East Asia. He is currently Director of the East Asia Nonproliferation Project of the Center for Nonproliferation Studies at the Monterey Institute of International Studies, California. His research focuses on arms trade, arms production and arms control in East Asia. His publications include *Chinese Arms Acquisitions from Abroad* (1995), *ASEAN Arms Acquisitions: Developing Transparency* (with J. N. Mak and S. T. Wezeman, 1995); *China's Arms Acquisitions from Abroad: A Quest for 'Superb and Secret Weapons'*, SIPRI Research Report no. 11 (with Taeho Kim, 1995); 'Arms acquisitions in East Asia', *SIPRI Yearbook 1994*; and *Chinese Arms Transfers* (1992). *Arming East Asia: Internationalization of the Region's Arms Trade and Production* is forthcoming as a SIPRI book.

Edward J. Laurance (USA) is Professor of International Policy Studies at the Monterey Institute of International Studies, California, where he also directs the Program for Arms Control, Disarmament and Conversion at the Center for Nonproliferation Studies. He is the author of *The International Arms Trade* (1992), co-author with H. Wulf and S. T. Wezeman of *Arms Watch: SIPRI Report on the First Year of the UN Register of Conventional Arms* (1993), and co-editor of *Developing the UN Register of Conventional*

Arms (1994). He is a member of the International Advisory Committee of the Arms Project of Human Rights Watch, and was consultant to the two expert groups which developed the UN Register of Conventional Arms.

J. N. Mak (Malaysia) is Director of Research at MIMA in Kuala Lumpur and head of its Maritime Security and Diplomacy Program. His research focuses on regional security matters with special emphasis on defence and naval affairs. He has published extensively on the subject in the *International Herald Tribune, Naval Forces,* the *Asia–Pacific Defence Reporter* and elsewhere. His recent publications include 'The ASEAN naval build-up: implications for regional order', *Pacific Review* (1995); and *ASEAN Arms Acquisitions: Developing Transparency* (with B. Gill and S. T. Wezeman, 1995).

Panitan Wattanayagorn (Thailand) heads the Defense Studies Program at the Institute of Security and International Studies in Bangkok and serves as a consultant to the Foreign Relations Committee of the Thai Senate. His research focuses on defence and arms trade issues in South-East Asia and has resulted in numerous articles and contributions to edited volumes. His recent publications include 'A regional arms race?' (with D. Ball), *Journal of Strategic Studies* (1995); and 'ASEAN's arms modernization and arms transfers', *Pacific Review* (1995). A book on the diversification of arms supply and indigenous arms production in ASEAN and a study with SIPRI on arms procurement decision making in Thailand are forthcoming.

Russ Swinnerton (Australia) was formerly the Defence Adviser to the Australian High Commission in Kuala Lumpur. His career as a naval officer has included operational staff positions with the Australian Defence Force. He was a visiting fellow at the Australian National University Strategic and Defence Studies Centre in 1994 and has published on such issues as UN peacekeeping operations and sea lines of communication. 'Confidence-building measures at sea: the challenges ahead in Southeast Asia' appeared in *Pacific Review* (1995).

Siemon T. Wezeman (The Netherlands) is a research assistant with the SIPRI Arms Transfers Project and a specialist on arms transfers and the UN Register of Conventional Arms. A regular contributor to the *SIPRI Yearbook,* he has published numerous articles on arms transfers; *ASEAN Arms Acquisitions: Developing Transparency* (with B. Gill and J. N. Mak, 1995); *1994 Arms Transfers: A Register of Deliveries from Public Sources* (with J. Sislin, 1995); and *Arms Watch: SIPRI Report on the First Year of the UN Register of Conventional Arms* (with E. Laurance and H. Wulf, 1993).

Index